D1070041

Fundamentally Flawed

Fundamentally Flawed

Understanding and Reforming Presidential Primaries

JOHN HASKELL

ROWMAN & LITTLEFIELD PUBLISHERS, INC.
Lanham • Boulder • New York • London

ROWMAN & LITTLEFIELD PUBLISHERS, INC.

Published in the United States of America
by Rowman & Littlefield Publishers, Inc.
4720 Boston Way, Lanham, Maryland 20706

3 Henrietta Street
London WC2E 8LU, England

British Cataloging in Publication Information Available

Library of Congress Cataloging-in-Publication Data

Haskell, John, 1959–
Fundamentally flawed: understanding and reforming presidential primaries /
John Haskell.
p. cm.
Includes bibliographical references and index.
1. Presidents—United States—Nomination. 2. Primaries—United States. I.
Title.
JK522.H376 1996 324.6'3'0972—dc20 96-7824 CIP

ISBN 0–8476–8240-4 (cloth : alk. paper)
ISBN 0–8476–8241-2 (pbk. : alk. paper)

Printed in the United States of America

♾™ The paper used in this publication meets the minimum requirements of
American National Standard for Information Sciences—Permanence of
Paper for Printed Library Materials, ANSI Z39.48–1984.

Contents

Tables

Preface

At this writing, in January 1996, the Republican presidential nomination campaign has already been going full steam for a year—and not a single delegate has been selected. In six weeks more than half of the delegates to the national convention will have been selected. In all likelihood, at that point or shortly thereafter, the Republican nominee will have been determined.

Never before has the public been forced to choose from such a long list of candidates in such a short period of time. Most of the primary voters will know little or nothing about most of the contenders when they vote. Now may mark the time in the history of American politics when the most uninformed choice for the most important office will have been made. This is the unhappy state of the presidential nomination process in the winter of 1996.

It is out of concern for the way presidents are selected today in the United States that the ideas for this book were spawned. It is my hope that the perspective and reforms presented here can contribute in some small way to generating more discussion about how the parties nominate presidential candidates.

Many people have contributed ideas and other sorts of help and advice that made this project possible. Discussions about presidential primaries with William Keech, Thad Beyle, Paul-Henri Gurian, and Kyoungsan Pak were very helpful in developing and revising my thinking. Jeffrey Russell was the source of the idea for the Geographical Balance Plan presented in chapter 8. William Farr and Donald Rasinen provided considerable research assistance, and Lynn Wellnitz was invaluable in editing and technical assistance.

This book would have been impossible without any one of these people, but it goes without saying that the author takes full responsibility for any and all errors on these pages.

Chapter One

Only in America

Casual observers of U.S. politics must be bewildered by the way that the Democratic and Republican parties nominate presidential candidates. Presidential nomination campaigns have developed into a confusing procession of primaries, caucuses, and state conventions, leading up to a pair of circuslike national party conventions. Very few Americans, attentive to politics or otherwise, can explain with any precision how this process works.

In the old days, more than a generation ago, American voters knew that the real determination of the parties' nominees was made at the national conventions, which were gatherings of the parties' insiders and power brokers. Today the conventions are carefully choreographed but largely meaningless media shows, which are appropriately ignored by most of the public and are covered much less thoroughly than before by the major mass media.

It is odd that the most important pair of decisions in U.S. electoral politics—who the major parties will nominate for president of the United States—is shrouded in such confusion, fully understood only by the candidates and their advisors, as well as a few scholars and journalists. Paradoxically the public is almost universally ignorant about a nomination campaign that is now dominated by events fully open to the participation of the public.

Presidential nomination campaigns in contemporary U.S. politics have evolved gradually over the course of the twentieth century into this Byzantine series of open and participatory primaries, caucuses, and conventions dominated by candidate-centered campaign organizations and no longer controlled by officials of the political parties. Serious candidates for a major party nomination must begin organizing their campaigns well in advance of the calendar year of the primaries. The public events, both the primaries and open precinct caucuses, are no longer just the testing grounds for potential candidacies as they were thirty or more years ago; instead, they are the places where the nominees of the major parties will be determined. These campaigns are probably the most complex and elaborate form of direct democracy ever developed. The full ramifications of such a process for nominating candidates for president are just now being fully explored.

Only in America

The way the major U.S. political parties nominate presidential candidates is truly distinctive. No other political party in the democratic countries of the world permits the kind of direct participation by its rank and file in the nomination of candidates for the chief executive position that the U.S. parties do. It should be re-emphasized that what makes the U.S. nomination process unique is not that there are avenues for participation by ordinary citizens but rather that ordinary citizens *actually determine the nominees.* For more than twenty years now the nominees from the two major parties (and, of course, every president in that time) have been produced by a form of direct democracy.

There is nothing necessarily wrong or controversial about a distinctive method of nominating candidates for the chief executive position, but there are important reasons why this process should receive much more careful and critical scrutiny than it does—perhaps more scrutiny than any other aspect of the electoral system.

The president of the United States is an incredibly powerful individual. Presidential nomination campaigns determine the momentous decision as to who, usually of the nominees of the two major parties, will be the next president. Nomination politics at other levels and branches of government are important as well. But if voters in primaries in a House district or Senate race nominate candidates who are poorly qualified and are of questionable character (as surely happens from time to time), the result is regrettable but hardly momentous. There are 435 members of the House and 100 senators. Any one member or senator cannot do irreparable harm to the nation (although a senator can be remarkably obstructive). And in our constitutional framework, the legislative branch as a whole, while tremendously powerful in the domestic sphere, can only do so much without being effectively checked .

But the U.S. president is different. He may not be able to reform welfare or pass health care reform or alter the tax code on a whim as the commander in chief of the only military superpower in the world, he has the virtually unchecked power to send U.S. troops and use U.S. military firepower anywhere on the globe at any time. (Included in that military firepower is a nuclear arsenal that can incinerate any city anywhere in the world in a matter of minutes.)

The presidential nomination process not only is open to the participation of the public but also is essentially open to any candidate with the ambition to be president and the resources to undertake a campaign. It is possible in such a system, for example, for the eventual nominee of one of the major parties to have been almost entirely unknown to the public just a few months prior to securing the nomination. In fact, the American public has twice in the past twenty years elected a president (Jimmy Carter in 1976 and Bill Clinton in 1992) who was largely unknown less than a year before the general election. Furthermore, these two candidates were nowhere near the top of the list of favored candidates of the elites in their parties until their eventual annointment as party standard-bearer was a foregone conclusion.

The fact is that a person can be elected president of the United States with a mandate from the public but without strong ties to the elites of the political party that nominated him. For all intents and purposes, the two major U.S. political parties effectively have eliminated any institutionalized form of peer review—that is, review by leaders within the party—in the selection of their presidential candidates. The presidential nomination process permits the possibility that the leader of the free world with the power of the world's greatest military force at his disposal can be selected entirely on the basis of a plebiscitary mandate.

Political Parties and Presidential Nomination Politics

It seems that every four years there is speculation by politicians and pundits alike that *this* will be the year of the first brokered or party-dominated convention in a generation or more. In the 1992 Democratic nomination race, for example, there was talk in February of the first brokered convention since 1952. The actively campaigning candidates were considered to be "second tier" figures within the party. None would be able to sustain a successful try at the nomination because of weak campaigns, moral flaws, or just general quirkiness, predicted the major politicians and pundits.

But, as with all races since 1972, the 1992 race once again was dominated by candidate-centered campaigns, with the regular party playing little or no role. The candidates who started campaigning before the calendar year of the election were the only ones with a realistic shot at winning enough delegates to secure the party's nomination. We saw again that tantalizing wait-and-see candidacies of the sort used by New York's Governor Mario Cuomo in 1992 (and to a lesser extent Congressman Richard Gephardt and Senator Lloyd Bentsen) are anachronisms. In an era in which the delegates to the national conventions (who vote to determine the nominees of the parties) are not controlled by party officials, but instead are controlled by the candidates themselves, it is reasonable to assume that candidacies such as Cuomo's always will be failures.

Why are presidential nomination campaigns like this in the United States? What has led to this unique style of democracy that has characterized our presidential campaigns?

To address these questions we need to take a step back to consider a theoretical issue regarding political parties in democratic polities. Political parties are described by political scientists as *intermediary institutions*. What this means is that the parties serve as the link between the people and the government. Probably the most important role political parties carry out in linking the people and the government is the process they go through to provide candidates for public office. Voters then choose from among the parties' candidates the person they prefer to serve a term in public office.

In this role and in others, political parties are indispensable for citizens in a democracy. But existing political parties must in theory continually earn their legitimacy as institutions acting on behalf of the public and serving in the public's interest. There are two *legitimate* ways in which political parties can choose candidates to run for office in democratic polities. The parties can legitimize their nomination processes by *representative* means or by *plebiscitary* means. These types of legitimacy entail:

Representative Legitimacy: Party leaders (sometimes called "regulars," "officials," or "elites") convene to select candidates for public office to carry the party label in the general election. Leaders may consult the rank and file members of the party to the extent they wish in the selection of the candidates, but ultimately the responsibility rests with the leadership to select worthy standard-bearers. In theory, the party retains its legitimacy to act for the people as long as the rank and file members believe that the leadership is doing an adequate job of selecting candidates.

Plebiscitary Legitimacy: The party uses participatory procedures, such as primary elections, to allow the rank and file to select from among a number of potential candidates to wear the party label in the general election. The theory is that opening the nomination process to the rank and file is the fairest way to select a nominee when more than one acceptable person wishes to be the party's candidate.

Presidential Nomination Politics in the Twentieth Century

The two major U.S. political parties, in the course of this century, have gradually drifted away from relying on representative means to legitimize their nomination procedures and now rely almost exclusively on plebiscitary means. And the type of plebiscitary legitimacy used is extreme, to say the least. The parties involve the public not just by permitting voters to determine the nominee from a list of candidates the party leaders deem acceptable; they actually go so far as to allow anyone's name to appear on the list of potential candidates, with almost no restrictions. This section looks briefly at how plebiscitary legitimacy became so deeply entrenched in the distinctive context of the development of U.S. political parties.

Political parties in the United States changed a great deal from about 1900 to the middle decades of the century. By mid-century civil service reforms (begun in many places during the Progressive era around the turn of the century) were nearly a ubiquitous aspect of U.S. state, local, and national politics, robbing political parties of the control of many patronage jobs. Already primaries had determined for decades both parties' nominees for many political offices in many states and locales across the nation, giving the people instead of party leaders final say over who the candidates would be. In that sense, *intraparty democracy* (another way of saying "plebiscitary legitimacy") was well entrenched at most levels of U.S. politics.

Presidential nominations, however, remained a partial exception. At mid-century party leaders retained a considerable measure of control over the national conventions at which the presidential candidates were nominated, but even by that time candidates running on their own frequently either challenged the parties' elites in the presidential primaries that took place in a few of the states, or they preempted the choice the elites might have made by vigorously courting them.

In the late 1960s and into the 1970s a powerful reform movement influenced the U.S. political process, in nearly all respects at all levels. The politics of the country became more open and more participatory, with less and less influence wielded at all levels by regular political party leaders. For example, in the early 1970s the proceedings of the U.S. Congress became open to public scrutiny to an extent never seen before, and the prerogatives of seniority were weakened as more members of Congress gained power through the increasingly important subcommittees. Even the actions of executive-branch bureaucrats became subject to congressional and public attention through sunshine and sunset laws and open hearings and other proceedings. A new culture of participation in the political process, best exemplified by the proliferation of direct democracy and of special interest groups, and often not expressed through the political parties, had taken firm root in the United States.

The Democratic and Republican parties adjusted to the *zeitgeist* of openness and reform accordingly. To retain their legitimacy they continued to move in the direction of opening up all of their procedures. It is probably the case that the two parties maintained their hegemony in U.S. politics *because* they opened up, gradually at first earlier in the century and at a quickening pace during the more recent reform movement starting in the late 1960s. Otherwise they might have been replaced or joined by other major parties.

Presidential nomination politics obviously did not exist in isolation from these other developments in the U.S. political system. Presidential politics was not immune to the larger social, cultural, and political trends affecting the rest of the political process, including the political parties.

Presidential nomination campaigns came to be dominated by open and plebiscitary procedures in time for the 1972 race, a hotly contested one on the Democratic side. The character of that campaign was new and distinctive, in part because of the efforts of reformers in the Democratic party who had become influential in the party's internal politics starting in about 1969. These reformers did not entirely understand or anticipate the way that presidential campaigns would change partly as a result of their actions. But it is important to note that the changes that they instituted were really just ratifications of developments in the direction of openness long in the making in U.S. politics and in the parties. Much more is said about this process of change in the next chapter.

Suffice it to say at this point that presidential nomination campaigns have become open to the involvement and participation of anyone—candidates and the public alike. Candidates for president succeed or fail in a process that is very nearly plebiscitary in character. The presidential nomination process has developed into a peculiar and distinctively American form of intraparty democracy.

To put it simply, the presidential nomination campaign has become a process of *public choice*. This book investigates the quality of that process.

Argument of the Book

There are important implications in viewing the nomination process as a method of public choice. Later chapters analyze this process of public choice from a couple of perspectives. One of these involves the use of a relatively recent development in the social sciences called *social choice theory*. Social choice theory enables one to analyze how fairly voters' preferences are aggregated and counted in an electoral procedure. This book examines what the basic tenets of social choice theory reveal about the fairness of the electoral procedures used in presidential nomination campaigns.

The fairness of electoral procedures obviously is important but the quality of a method of public choice rests on more than technical issues. The quality of the decision making and discourse during the campaign also must be considered. In doing so the book addresses the following questions: In the course of the campaign, does the public have the reasonable opportunity carefully to scrutinize the candidates running in the race; do the candidates have the opportunity to learn the concerns of the public? Does the public have the chance to reconsider hastily made judgments about the major contenders? Is the nomination race accessible enough to candidates such that the rigors of the campaign do not discourage worthy people from running?

If the United States is to have intraparty plebiscitary democracy in presidential campaigns, the procedure first must be fair, of course, but it also must allow the voters the chance to learn the positions and accomplishments of the candidates, as well as provide the opportunity for judgments to be made about character. This book looks at the specific electoral arrangements in, as well as the dynamics of, presidential nomination campaigns; it proceeds from there to analyze the quality of the process as a form of public choice.

Ultimately, the current arrangements in the presidential nomination process are deeply flawed, particularly with the pronounced trend toward frontloading primaries early in the campaign season. The electoral procedures violate basic tenets of democratic fairness, as can be seen by employing rudimentary tools of social choice theory. And the contemporary campaign environment, produced in part by the current arrangements, may be less and less conducive to reasoned discourse and responsible decision making.

Many popular reform alternatives, such as a national primary, offer no panacea, however, and may in some cases exacerbate existing problems. The case is made at the end of the book that carefully targeted reforms can address the more serious flaws in the way parties currently go about nominating presidential candidates.

Plan of the Book

This book serves both as a basic text for understanding how the contemporary presidential nomination process evolved and as an introduction to the study of the presidential nomination process as a method of public choice. To aid in the analysis of the quality of this process of public choice, the reader is introduced to some nontechnical, analytical tools of social choice theory. Major proposals for the reform of the process also are discussed and subjected to analysis. It concludes with some original reform proposals that apply lessons drawn from the public choice analysis to the nomination process.

In the first section of the book, chapters 2, 3 and 4 look at the historical developments that led to the current arrangements in presidential nomination campaigns. In chapter 2, the major changes in the political parties through the course of this century that eventually led to the endorsement of plebiscitary legitimacy by the parties are chronicled. In chapter 3, the nature of the contemporary process is described in detail, including recent developments that have altered the landscape for the 1996 campaign. Case studies from recent campaigns in the 1980s and the 1992 campaign are used to illustrate the details and dynamics of the nomination process. Chapter 4 covers the debates that have raged in recent years over the merits of the current process as a way to go about choosing the nominees for president of the United States. Also in that chapter, some major proposals (a national primary, regional primaries, for example) to overhaul the existing structure of primaries and caucuses are described.

In the second section of the book, chapters 5, 6, and 7 introduce the basic elements of public choice analysis as they apply to presidential nomination campaigns. Chapter 5 looks at the concept of social choice theory and develops a simple set of criteria by which to assess the technical fairness of an electoral procedure such as presidential primaries. In chapter 6 the current arrangements in the presidential nomination process are subjected to analysis by these criteria. Next, chapter 7 looks again at the popular reform proposals to see how they stack up against the current process as a way to select presidential candidates.

Finally, chapter 8 presents a set of original reform alternatives that address the major shortcomings of the presidential nomination process.

Chapter Two

The Twentieth-Century Evolution of the Presidential Nomination Process

The term *presidential nomination process* simply means the procedures that the two major political parties use to nominate candidates for the presidency. As touched on in the first chapter, the parties and the presidential nomination process underwent profound changes during the course of this century.

These changes turned the parties into the participatory institutions they are today, open to the influence of the interested public, quite unlike the closed and sometimes rather autocratic institutions they once were. Whereas parties once were controlled by party leaders or regulars who doled out patronage and determined the makeup of the party ticket, today the party leadership has far less power and is far less important during nomination campaigns than the organizations formed by the individual candidates in hot pursuit of public office. Parties have taken on the ancillary, although not inconsequential, role of assisting in general elections candidates who already have won the party's nomination in open competition with other candidates. Later sections address how and why this profound change in how the parties go about their business took place and how it affected presidential nomination politics.

The main focus in this chapter is on the development and the codification of the contemporary, largely plebiscitary, presidential nomination process. To understand the nomination process, it is necessary to look back at the changes made in the party system around the turn of the century during the Progressive era. These changes, for all intents and purposes, started the political parties on the road to their current state as more open and participatory institutions. We then look at some of the technological developments in mid-century that affected the political parties, particularly in communications and in public opinion polling. These developments facilitated the formation of the candidate-centered campaign organizations that forever changed the face of nomination politics. Subsequent sections consider the ramifications of the tumult of the 1960s on the nomination process. Finally, this chapter looks at how some of the changes in campaign finance rules in the 1970s had an impact on the process.

The Decline of Parties

Revolutionary changes in the party system in the direction of increased openness in intraparty politics took place around the turn of the century because of the reforms associated with the Progressive movement, but presidential nomination politics in those days remained almost entirely in the control of state and county party officials for the first few decades of the century. Lester Seligman and Cary Covington (1989) argue that party leaders finally began gradually to lose their grip on presidential nominations in the 1930s. Howard Reiter (1985) demonstrates empirically the way that the process began to slip from the hold of state and local party leaders beginning in the 1950s. (His findings are summarized in the section entitled "Change at Mid-Century.")

But the seeds of change in the social and political context of the country, leading to the weakening of the power of the organizational party in presidential nomination politics, date back to the Progressive reforms. Most important, it was the reformist *ideas* of the Progressives that had a lasting legacy on all of the major institutions in U.S. politics.

The Progressive movement had a broad-based reform agenda involving a myriad of social and economic concerns, but one of its main objectives was undermining the strength of the party machines. Political party leaders in many states, counties, and cities controlled the politics and the lives of their communities. They mobilized the vote on election day with promises of jobs, relief, and other public services—and they could deliver. Party leaders controlled all government jobs in some areas, doled out contracts (frequently taking kickbacks as part of "doing business"), controlled social welfare expenditures and the distribution of services, and often influenced the outcomes of elections through various sorts of fraud and inventive vote counting.

The reform agenda at around the turn of the century focused on the abuses of the party leaders, the election fraud, kickbacks, nepotism, and the like. Progressives, the leaders of the reform movement, usually were found in the Republican party and were made up disproportionately of better-educated elites. Although one of the Progressives' motives surely was to regain political power for these predominantly white Anglo-Saxon Protestant elites—power that had been lost to immigrant groups in some cities—they relied on (and believed in) persuasive theoretical arguments to make their case against strong parties and the rampant fraud in so many places perpetrated by some of the party bosses.

They believed that these powerful party leaders (the bosses) held too much power over politicians and citizens. "[E]ach citizen shall for himself exercise his choice by direct vote, without the intervention or interference of any political agency," said Wisconsin Progressive Robert LaFollette, who ran one of the most successful third-party presidential campaigns in history under the Progressive banner in 1924 (Ranney 1975, 124). LaFollette and other Progressives believed that parties would be strengthened by their purification. Some went even further.

George W. Norris of Nebraska, for example, said that a decrease in partisanship would be a healthy development, leading to better, more open, and certainly more honest government (Ranney 1978, 24).

The result of the successes of the Progressive era of reform was that many local party organizations of the traditional boss-dominated sort described above were weakened or undermined. A variety of methods was used to achieve that end by the reformers. Strict voter registration and the introduction of the secret ballot and ballots more conducive to split-ticket voting hurt the parties' ability to control or influence outcomes at the ballot box. Redistricting and at-large districts engineered by Progressives and rural interests hurt the bosses vis-à-vis their rural and WASP-elite competitors for power in statehouses and municipal governments. Stricter government auditing procedures cast many powerful politicians in a bad light because of corruption in some of the local party organizations. Civil service reforms reduced the number of jobs that parties could dole out to the faithful. The introduction of primary elections undermined the central and critical role of determining candidate nominations at the state and local levels. Also, governments in more and more places began usurping some of the traditional roles of the parties in the dispensation of welfare and in the provision of various municipal services.

As a result of all these changes, Americans' strong traditional allegiances to parties gradually began to erode as early as the second decade of the twentieth century. Simply put, parties and the people in leadership positions in many parts of the country began to lose their hold over the people, probably reducing the psychological attachment that many people had to a party. Walter Dean Burnham (1970) found that ever since the Progressive era there has been a steady decline in straight-ticket voting in many parts of the country, with the exception of some upsurge in the 1930s. Even the New Deal realignment occurring at that time in favor of the Democrats, from the presidential to local levels of government, took much longer to complete than ones prior to the reforms that made split-ticket voting possible.

Shortly after the Progressive era, technological changes in mass communications further weakened the traditional links between the parties and their rank and file. The advent of radio in the 1920s almost immediately permitted politicians to develop a type of personal rapport with voters that was impossible before. The first to make that connection was President Calvin Coolidge, who arguably successfully appealed to people over the heads of Republican power brokers to ensure his nomination in 1924 (Milkis and Nelson 1990, 251). Of course, Franklin Roosevelt and subsequent presidents and contenders have continued to exploit and refine Coolidge's "invention." Essentially, changes in communications technology allowed politicians easier direct contact with voters, exacerbating the trend in the direction of voters' independence from the parties. Voters more and more felt comfortable "voting for the man," instead of for the party.

Changes at Mid-Century

Losing the Grip on the Delegates

To understand how the changes of the Progressive era altered presidential nomination campaigns, a short detour is necessary to explain the most fundamental components of the nomination of presidential candidates in U.S. politics.

The fundamentals are rather simple:

1. To win the nomination of a major party, a candidate must receive the vote of a majority (fifty percent plus one) of his party's delegates at the quadrennial national convention, held the summer of the presidential election year. (For a time the Democrats required a 2/3 special majority; this was changed in 1936.)

2. The national convention delegation is comprised of fifty state party delegations and delegations from the District of Columbia and some of the territories.

3. The state parties determine how to select their delegates for the national convention, subject to national party rules.

At this most fundamental level, presidential nomination politics is easy to understand. When trying to gain a sophisticated understanding of the outcome of a presidential nomination race, the central fact that must be focused on is how the states go about selecting their delegates to the national conventions. The vote of the delegates determines the nominee of the party. What matters, then, is how these delegates are selected in the state and whether the delegates are given a free rein to vote as they please at the convention.

Basically, over the course of most of U.S. history, states have used either primary elections or party meetings (the "caucus/convention system"), or some combination of the two, to select their delegates to the national convention. State primaries did not dominate nomination politics for the presidency by mid-century as they had begun to dominate nomination politics for other offices, but changes in the nature of presidential nomination politics were evident by that time. Delegate selection to the national party conventions and the delegates themselves were becoming less tightly controlled by the state and local organizational parties, consistent with the weakening of the organizational party in other respects that began in the Progressive era. This was true even though most of the delegates to the national conventions up until 1972 were selected via the caucus/convention system of party meetings.

Howard Reiter developed a set of measures to assess the extent to which party leaders have controlled delegates and the nominating conventions over the last century or so. His thesis is that party leaders in the states gradually lost control of state delegations that historically had voted in lockstep with the wishes of these powerful party regulars. The Democratic party instituted rules changes in the early 1970s that resulted in a dramatic increase in the use of primaries to select delegates and to guide their voting at the national conventions. (Delegates selected on the basis of primaries are much more likely to be selected explicitly to support a specific active candidate and consequently are much less likely to be controlled at the convention by the party leadership.) But Reiter's point is that even before the proliferation of primaries in the states to select and instruct their delegates, the party leadership had lost control over many of the delegates—with delegates increasingly acting either as free agents or functioning under the control of candidates rather than the party.

Essentially he is saying that the rules changes that the Democrats instituted around 1970 merely codified, and did not cause, the weakening of the control of party leaders over state delegations in presidential nomination politics. The following is a summary of some of his findings and his measures of party strength in presidential nomination politics, documenting the gradual loss of control over delegates by the parties noticeable by mid-century, long before the spate of reforms in the 1970s.

Measure #1, Number of Uncommitted Delegates

We would assume that a fewer number of delegates previously uncommitted to any specific candidate at the national conventions would indicate that delegation leaders—the party leaders—would have less leeway to negotiate during the convention. This would decrease the party leaders' power, control, and influence at the convention. Uncommitted delegates could be used as bargaining chips by the leadership of a state's delegation, perhaps to engineer the nomination of candidate preferred by the leadership in the state.

Measure #2, Favorite Son Candidates

A decrease in the number of favorite son candidacies (candidacies of home state politicians) also would indicate a lack of power and bargaining leverage on the part of the leadership. Favorite son candidacies were a traditional means used by party leaders to maintain bargaining leverage at conventions. The "favorite sons" usually were not serious presidential candidates but rather lent their names to be used at the convention to keep the state's delegation independent.

Measure #3, Unit Votes

A decline in the number of unit votes (state delegations voting as a bloc for one candidate) would indicate a lack of control by power brokers. Traditionally party leaders could use their entire delegation for bargaining leverage, since they could force the delegation to vote as a bloc.

Measure #4, Multiple Ballot Conventions

A decline in the number of multiple ballot conventions would indicate a lack of leadership control. Surely if party power brokers maintained control, enough would not play all their cards on the first ballot in order to exercise bargaining leverage on later ballots.

Table 2.1 shows that the decline in the number of uncommitted delegates has been evident throughout the period depicted (it is difficult to get reliable information on uncommitted delegates prior to 1952) and in both parties already was quite low by the 1960s. This indicates that the decline in the uncommitteds was not just a function of the rules changes instituted by the Democrats after 1968. Party leaders increasingly were unable to hold delegations uncommitted at the conventions by the 1960s and consequently were unable to exercise the kind of control they once were able to in the decision making at the convention.

Table 2.2 shows that the number of favorite son candidacies (defined as candidates receiving less than 10 percent of the votes at the convention roll call) also has been low and has been constantly low since the 1950s. State party leaders either have found it fruitless to try to delay the decision making at the conventions by the use of favorite son candidacies because it is evident that the front-runner cannot be stopped or simply have not been able to rely on their delegations to support them in such an effort.

Table 2.3 shows that the percentage of state delegations voting as a unit began to decline starting in 1952, with the drop particularly noticeable on the Democratic side. The data is far less conclusive on the Republican side. The change for the Democrats is important because it was not until after 1968 that the party outlawed unit voting. Again, the control over the delegations by the leaders appears to have begun to weaken before the rules changes accelerated the decline in the 1970s.

With regard to measure #4, there has not been a multiple ballot convention since 1952 for the Democrats and 1948 for the Republicans. There have been many hotly contested conventions since the 1950s, but no front-runner has been denied a victory on the first ballot. If more party delegation leaders would have had more control over their delegations, it is quite likely that at some point, to gain bargaining leverage, they would have withheld enough support from a front runner to deny him a first ballot nomination.

All of these trends indicate the effects of the decline of the organizational party's controlling influence in nomination politics. The organizational party's decreasing role was evident long before the reforms of the 1970s. By the middle of the century party leaders no longer exercised control over the decision making at the conventions to the extent that they had before—although they did manage to prevail on the Democratic side in both 1952 and 1968.

Table 2.1
Percentage of delegates uncommitted the weekend before each contested convention, 1952-84

Year	Percentage	Source
Democrats		
1952	29.3	*New York Times*, July 20, 1952, section 1, p. 34
1956	27.8	*New York Times*, August 13, 1956, p. 13
1960	24.2	*Washington Post*, July 10, 1960, p. A6
1968	11.9	*New York Times*, August 25, 1968, sec. 1, p. 1
1972	7.3	*Washington Post*, July 9, 1972, p. A2
1980	3.1	*Washington Post*, August 10, 1980, p. C5
Republicans		
1952	9.8	*New York Times*, July 6, 1952, sec. 1, p. 36
1964	15.4	*New York Times*, July 12, 1964, sec. 1, p. 57
1968	3.8	*New York Times*, August 4, 1968, sec. 1, p. 1
1976	4.7	*New York Times*, August 15, 1976, sec. 1, p. 24

Source: Reiter, H. (1985) *Selecting the President* (Philadelphia: University of Pennsylvania Press), p. 26.

Table 2.2
Percentage of votes on first ballots of contested conventions going to candidates who individually received less than 10 percent of the vote, 1896-1984

Year	Democratic	Republican
1896	49.6	-
1904	14.2	-
1912	5.9	6.2*
1916	-	53.2
1920	40.2	35.7
1924	38.8	-
1932	24.8	-
1940	-	34.6
1948	3.4	25.5
1952	18.3	9.2
1956	18.7	-
1960	20.1	-
1964	-	16.1
1968	10.0	13.7
1972	12.6	-
1976	11.9	0.1
1980	1.7	-
1984	0.7	-

*Not including votes for Theodore Roosevelt or abstentions.

Source: Reiter, H. (1985) *Selecting the President* (Philadelphia: University of Pennsylvania Press), p. 28.

Table 2.3
Percentage of Democratic delegations voting unanimously at contested conventions, 1896-1984

Year	Percentage
1896	60.0
1904	80.0
1912	72.9
1920	45.8
1924	77.1
1932	85.4
1948	83.3
1952	50.0
1956	54.2
1960	58.0
1968	6.0
1972	14.0
1976	12.0
1980	4.0
1984	2.0

Source: Reiter, H. (1985) *Selecting the President* (Philadelphia: University of Pennsylvania Press) p. 74.

So who, if anyone, was controlling or influencing delegates at the national party conventions if not party leaders? Were the delegates acting independently, exercising their individual judgment as "trustees" rather than "delegates" in deciding how to vote? Probably not in most cases. What was happening was that delegates, *and even sometimes the party leaders,* increasingly were becoming tied to candidates and the candidates' organizations instead of to the traditional party organizations.

Candidate-Centered Campaign Organizations

What accounts for this trend in delegates' allegiances toward candidates instead of the party leadership in their state or local organization? For the first time, in the middle of the century, candidates began to form their own campaign organizations independent of the organizational party at the state, local, or national levels. President Franklin Roosevelt did this in 1936 (Seligman and Covington 1989), and Wendell Willkie's successful nomination campaign in 1940 was done with an insurgent candidate-centered movement. Long before the proliferation of primaries in the 1970s, Dwight Eisenhower, Estes Kefauver, John Kennedy, and Barry Goldwater either wooed party leaders independently or filled the delegate selection processes in the states (again, usually caucus/convention meetings) with amateur insurgents in an effort to preempt whatever choice traditional power brokers might have made if left to their own devices. Of course, Eisenhower, Kennedy, and Goldwater were successful in doing so, securing their parties' nominations in 1952, 1960, and 1964, respectively.

Advances in communications and transportation technology, and the concomitant breakdown of some of the power of the party organizations, enabled candidates to reach delegates and state and local officials directly. Candidates increasingly were actively campaigning for support among party officials and delegates alike. With the potential nominees all out seeking support, it became impossible for much of the leadership to withhold support. Perhaps as early as 1940, and certainly by the 1950s, the party organization leaders (presiding over their gradually atrophying organizations) were reduced to the role of handicappers instead of kingmakers during the nomination campaigns. As Reiter's data suggest, waiting on the sidelines until the convention no longer was a feasible strategy for the leadership.

A good example is the 1960 Democratic race. In that year, many party leaders on the Democratic side found themselves as handicappers, deciding whether to throw their weight behind a force (the Kennedy candidacy) they might not be able to stop. Most of Kennedy's competitors were a bit behind the times. Chief among these was Senate Majority Leader Lyndon Johnson. He thought his strength among insiders would be enough to stop Kennedy on the first ballot at the convention. Johnson theorized that a deadlocked convention would put him in a position to win in subsequent balloting. But Kennedy and other active candidates had preempted the candidacy of Johnson by forcing the hand of the delegates and the leadership by securing commitments long before the convention. Johnson's assessment of the nature of presidential nomination politics was outdated.

Perhaps the best example of an insurgent candidacy infiltrating the delegate selection process was the Barry Goldwater campaign in 1964. Goldwater's campaign is distinguishable from other successful candidate organizations around this time because his candidacy was actively opposed by many of the most powerful and influential people in the party. (Eisenhower, Kennedy, and Willkie, while succeeding with organizations largely independent of their parties, generally were popular with the established leadership.)

Not at all the favorite of most of the Republican party's organizational leaders around the country, Goldwater and his strategists brilliantly drummed up grass roots support around the country—particularly in strategically located states where party organizations were more permeable or relatively new. The delegate selection process in the southern states, on the GOP side, was especially open to insurgency in those days, since the southern states had had a very weak (essentially nonexistent in some places) Republican organizational structure. Goldwater's people dominated these states with the permeable party structures and squeaked out a victory at the convention, much to the chagrin of the party's so-called Old Guard. This achievement was a testament to the openness and permeability of party structures in the United States even at that time, something not well understood by Goldwater's competitors for the nomination.

Plebiscitary Democracy? Not Quite Yet

One of the reasons the Goldwater success was so exceptional was that candidates in mid-century still found themselves competing for most of the delegates in state party meetings that usually were not permeable to insurgent movements actively opposed by the leadership. There were a limited number of states that held primaries in those days—usually about fifteen to seventeen. And many of these primaries were only "beauty contests," that is, they were not the means by which the state selected delegates, rather they were simply a means used by the party leaders to gauge the views of its rank and file.

It was the case through the middle years of the century, however, that most candidates deemed it necessary to make a good showing in some of the primaries, even though these events were not decisive in terms of securing enough delegates for the nomination. Only rarely did candidates feel secure enough to avoid the primaries—and the potential embarrassment of a loss—altogether. Why did candidates feel compelled to contest the primaries?

For the lesser-known or insurgent candidate, it was a chance to gain publicity. For some, it was a chance to demonstrate vote-getting ability. But perhaps most importantly in a democracy with a national election looming a few months in the future, primaries were a good opportunity for party leaders to gauge the feelings of the public. Certainly any candidate who avoided primaries could be made to look as though he were running scared. The party leaders—who as was noted were fast becoming handicappers instead of kingmakers—could handicap better if they knew something of the support a candidate had among the rank and file.

There was another development in mid-century that added a popular component to the nomination process. This was the advent of scientific public opinion polling, first used in U.S. politics in the 1930s. The increasing popular component of so many of the campaigns (with independent campaign organizations and primary elections) forced the leaders of the party organizations to consult the polls.

Frequently since sophisticated polling was invented in the 1930s, as William Keech and Donald Matthews (1974) have shown, the leadership seemed to go along with the popular choice. Unless the front-running candidate had some obvious flaws, the path of least resistance for state and local party leaders was to encourage their delegations (some still had a substantial measure of influence, if not actually control, over them) to support the leader in the polls. It probably is fair to say that as long as there was a substantial popular element to the campaigns, democratic politicians instinctively relied to a significant extent on popular opinion. The leadership would assert its representative role if the choice of the people in primaries or in the polls was too noxious, but more often than not they found it wise to acquiesce to public opinion.

To summarize, presidential nomination politics had changed a good deal by the 1950s and 1960s in the long wake of the reforms of the Progressive era. No longer were all the delegates selected in closed party meetings and controlled at the convention by party power brokers. Primaries and public opinion polling had lent an explicitly popular component to the campaigns. In a country in which democratic ideals are as much an article of faith as they are in the United States, this popular component also often was irresistible to the elite leadership class of the parties.

The most telling change in presidential nomination politics involved a confluence of factors. The loosening of the grip of the party leaders on their fiefdoms left an opening for the candidates. Technological changes gave candidates the opportunity to reach delegates, party leaders, and voters directly. And the candidates, as early as Franklin Roosevelt in the 1930s, formed their own sophisticated campaign organizations to exploit the new opportunities.

By and large, from early in the century up into the 1960s, for both parties, the delegate selection process gradually was becoming more open in more states. The party leadership's position had atrophied to the extent that it was unable to act as the unchallenged kingmaker. (This is not to say that historically the leadership always spoke with one voice. This was manifestly not the case. Bargaining and negotiating among the elites always had characterized convention politics, particularly on the Democratic side, where the intraparty regional differences were especially profound.) There was enough party control in most cases for the leaders to exert veto power over politicians they regarded as dangerous candidates, the Republican 1964 example being the glaring exception.

Instead, the process had evolved to the extent that most candidates were on their own to gather support in the various state delegate selection events and impress powerful people with strong showings in the primaries. The leadership would weigh in, but for the most part as a reaction to the campaigning being carried on by independent candidate organizations. They were now handicappers, throwing their weight behind candidates who seemed to be a good bet. Generally, the leadership was not able to determine the nominee at the convention. Too much was going on publicly before the conventions, with all the polling and primaries, to be controlled by the leadership, and increasingly the delegates were not controllable by the old power brokers.

By the 1960s the general tone of today's nomination process had been set. Candidates had to start out early and win delegates on their own with their own campaign organization with or without strong ties to the institutional party. Candidates could not rely on assurances from influential people in the party to carry the day at the convention; fewer and fewer state party leaders could be depended on to control their state's delegation as fewer and fewer of the delegates were uncommitted when the convention convened.

From fund-raising, to generating amateur activity, to cultivating the media, to hiring professional consultants, many of the campaigns of the 1950s and 1960s required the same sort of effort as the contemporary ones do.

Late 1960s, Early 1970s—The End of Party Influence

As in the rest of the political process, openness and participation were coming to the parties in presidential politics. The leadership could not pursue its aims unchallenged by insurgent forces rallying around independent campaign organizations.

Even so, the 1968 Democratic convention looked in some ways like an old-time convention controlled by elements of the organizational party unmoved by the sentiments of the public as expressed in primaries and polls. Nineteen-sixty-eight was a very tumultuous year in many ways, both political and cultural, reflected as much within the Democratic party as almost anywhere in society. The party was split in at least three ways: an anti-Vietnam War faction that was represented by Senators Eugene McCarthy and Robert Kennedy (who was assassinated two months before the convention); a southern conservative faction that was resistant to the economic, racial, and social liberalism of the rest of the party—it was represented by Governor George Wallace, who left the party that year to run for president as an independent; and the labor-dominated party establishment, still loyal to President Lyndon Johnson and supportive of the presidential candidacy of Vice President Hubert Humphrey after Johnson removed himself from consideration for renomination.

Just like old times, the party leadership supportive of Humphrey held sway at the convention. But in other ways this was a convention like no other, and it was a harbinger of major changes in the nomination process. The opposition to the party establishment coming from the antiwar faction was openly expressed and at times ruthlessly suppressed within the convention hall in Chicago, as well as out in the streets of the city. As a direct result of the protests of the losers at the convention (from among the ranks of the antiwar wing of the party), rule changes were made within the party, ratifying and codifying open and participatory presidential nomination politics for the Democrats. An *explicitly* plebiscitary form of nomination politics would replace the vestiges of representative decision making by organizational party leaders that still existed in states, counties, and cities.

The genesis of reform politics in 1968 came mostly from the supporters of insurgent presidential candidate Eugene McCarthy. At the convention, reform-minded Democrats proposed resolutions calling for future commissions to study the delegate selection process and the relationship between the state and national party organizations. Their efforts were inspired by the heavy-handed treatment supporters of McCarthy and other nonestablishment candidates received at party caucuses and party conventions in many states around the country during the process of delegate selection in the spring of 1968. In essence, many McCarthy supporters were excluded from any meaningful participation at some of these meetings. Some of the resolutions passed at the convention created commissions (to convene before the 1972 campaign) for the study of delegate selection procedures used by the state Democratic parties.

Byron Shafer (1983) believes that these resolutions were allowed to succeed by the party regulars (who, remember, dominated the '68 convention) because of the regulars' traditional coalitional, accommodating approach to dealing with intraparty differences. This was a party long used to dealing with major rifts in the ranks and well practiced in the art of compromise and conciliation. The regulars probably believed that the resolutions were insignificant—a bone thrown to the so-called New Politics wing of the party represented by the McCarthy supporters and some former Kennedy supporters. Shafer says that the same approach applied when the first round of recommendations for change came from the first of the reform commissions in 1969. The regular party leadership (headed by Larry O'Brien) went along with the recommendations of the first reform commission, refusing or unable to see the extent to which the changes would affect their positions of power.

What happened in the Democratic party was truly, in Shafer's words, a "quiet revolution." The reformers within the party, mostly white, middle class, and well educated, and liberal across the board, especially so on social and cultural issues but generally less so on economic questions, became very powerful within the Democratic party in a relatively short period of time. In fact, this faction of the party seemed successfully to wrest control of the workings of the party from the labor-dominated wing that supported Humphrey in 1968. For all practical purposes, they managed to get the concept of reassessing delegate selection rules between the quadrennial conventions institutionalized, as further reform commissions were created in the 1970s and 1980s.

The most consequential of the reform commissions was the McGovern-Fraser Commission in 1970. This commission dictated several new national party rules that from that point forward would govern delegate selection procedures in the states. Of these rules, two were particularly important.

1. Delegates to the national Democratic convention can be selected in the states either on the basis of primary elections or through a caucus/convention system of party meetings, during which the initial phase (precinct caucuses) is publicly advertised and open to full participation by the rank and file. It is important to note there must be a direct connection between these events open to public participation and the selection of delegates.

2. State delegations must have a racial makeup proportional to the state's Democratic racial makeup; women must be proportionally represented; people thirty and under must be proportionally represented.

The large numbers of primaries that characterized the nomination process since 1972 are an indirect result of these reforms (see table 2.4). Although these early reform commissions before the 1972 convention specifically stipulated only that the opportunity to participate in nomination politics be enhanced and made generally available, there was rhetoric to encourage the adoption of primaries. For example, the Hughes Commission (1969) stated that the failure of some states to use primaries to select delegates was acceptable only if it did not undercut the firm commitment Democrats have for direct democracy in presidential nomination campaigns.

Table 2.4
Total number of primaries

Year	Democrats # of Primaries	Republicans # of Primaries
1960	18	17
1964	18	18
1968	17	16
1972	23	23
1976	31	29

Some of the participants in the reform commissions, such as political scientist Austin Ranney, contended that the proliferation of primaries that ensued was not intentional. But the reformers, while not explicitly stating a plebiscitary expectation, did specify that the role of rank-and-file opinion should supersede that of the major interest blocs that had dominated the party in the days of the control of the strongly pro-labor party establishment.

In any event, the fact is that the result of the first of the McGovern-Fraser reforms listed above was more primaries to select delegates. There were a couple of reasons that the requirement that precinct caucus meetings be open led to more primaries. First, many of the state party organizational leaders decided that only through primaries could their delegations avoid credentials challenges at the national convention given the variety of more stringent rules the reformers created in the commissions governing how delegations could be selected through the caucus/convention procedure.

Also, there was some feeling that insurgent radical amateurs from the antiwar wing of the party (who were opposed by the party regulars for the most part) would fare worse in primaries than they would in caucuses that now would have to be advertised and open. The reason for this fear was well-founded. The establishment leaders hypothesized that caucuses would be sparsely attended compared to the voting turnout in primaries. Consequently it would be relatively easy for a well-organized fringe candidate to rally his troops and overwhelm caucus meetings, resulting in the selection of large numbers of delegates favorable to his candidacy. The broader mass of rank-and-file Democrats, whom they figured to be unsympathetic to liberal or radical reform candidates, would show up in larger numbers in primaries, thus diluting the turnout of the committed group of supporters of the fringe candidate.

The worries of the party regulars have been borne out in nomination campaigns since the advent of the requirement for open precinct caucuses. The darling of the 1972 antiwar movement, Senator George McGovern, did far better in states that selected delegates with the caucus/convention system of relatively sparsely attended party meetings than in those states with primaries. There are other examples of candidates (in both parties) with more extreme views and committed followings doing better in open caucuses. Reverend Jesse Jackson had some of his most impressive successes in caucus states in 1988. On the Republican side, Reverend Pat Robertson startled the nation by finishing second, ahead of Vice President George Bush, in the 1988 Iowa precinct caucuses.

So Democratic politicians around the country in the early 1970s, where they could, legislated presidential primaries in their states. The result was the dramatic upswing in the number of primaries between 1968 and 1972 and the continued increase between 1972 and 1976. Actually, the figures on the number of primaries (table 2.4) underestimates the nature of the change in the nomination process. Many of the delegates in states holding primaries before 1972 were not tightly bound, or even bound at all, to the candidates competing in the primaries. Delegates selected in primaries after the rule changes were far more likely than before to have what James Ceaser (1979) calls a "national candidate orientation," instead of a more local connection with the state party unit. This means that delegates selected in primaries were more likely after 1972 to maintain an allegiance to one of the candidates in the primary than to state or local organizational party leaders.

The establishment wing of the party that successfully secured the nomination of Humphrey (against intense and extremely vocal minority opposition) at the 1968 Chicago convention was having its grip on the nomination process loosened and ultimately removed. The choice between primaries and open caucuses may have been an easy one for many of the state leaders, but it was not a particularly good choice for them. Primaries obviously were better for them, but their favorite choice for delegate selection—caucus meetings that they could control if necessary—was not one of the options. Delegates would be selected based on the support in their state (either expressed through primaries or open party meetings) for a national presidential candidate. State and local party leadership control of delegates was effectively gone. Their best hope was that the people in primaries would select the candidate they favored.

To add insult to injury, the second of the major reforms recommended by the McGovern-Fraser Commission—the quota system for state delegations—further tied the hands of state and local leadership. In many cases, to meet the quota requirements, outsiders would have to be let into the state's delegation to the national convention.

The best illustration of this predicament for the Democratic party leadership was the situation of the Cook County (Chicago) contingent of the Illinois delegation to the 1972 convention. The local organizational party was as strong, and maybe stronger, there as in any other place in the country. The traditional Cook County contingent, made up primarily of white ethnic Democrats (mostly men) with strong ties to organized labor and/or county government, was challenged that year, partly on the basis of the new quota rules, by a rump group of racially diverse potential delegates led by Reverend Jesse Jackson. The national party, as expressed by a vote of all delegates at the 1972 national convention, ruled in favor of the rump group, a battle ultimately fought out in the courts. The courts ruled that the national party had and could enforce its delegate selection rules on the state delegations. In effect, in this case, in the realm of presidential nomination politics, the backbone of the organizational party had been broken in its strongest place.

The bonds between delegates and the party leaders became progressively weaker—and usually the bonds between delegates and national candidates for president became progressively stronger—with rule changes instituted by the Mikulski and Winograd Commissions in the 1970s.

Most important among these changes (really additions to the McGovern-Fraser Commission changes) was Candidates' Right of Approval (CRA "Candidates' Right of Approval\; (CRA.i.Candidates' Right of Approval"), established by the Winograd Commission. This reform gave candidates the right to reject delegates unsatisfactory to them who originally were selected in the states to support them. In fact, candidates have never exercised this power, because state parties usually permit the candidates (in accordance with national rules) the power to arrange their own slates of delegates dependent on their success in primaries and caucuses. Nonetheless, CRA is important because of the effect it has in codifying the orientation and connection of the delegates toward the national presidential candidates and *not* toward the state and local party leaders.

Furthermore, many state parties have adopted rules in accordance with the spirit of the national party commissions that bind primary and caucus delegates to the candidate they originally were selected to represent for at least one ballot at the national convention. All of these rules add up to the further diminution of the role of the organizational party leadership in the nomination of presidential candidates and the accretion of the role of candidate-centered organizations.

Democrats, in their reform panels, have gone so far as to include language in their delegate selection rules to indicate that delegates should be chosen to represent some conception of a fair reflection of candidate preferences as expressed in these primaries and open caucus/convention processes. This has taken the form, off and on over the last twenty years, of mandating proportional allocation of delegates based on the results of the delegate selection events held in the states. Once the national Democratic party even voted at one of its conventions (1980) officially to bind all of its delegates to the candidate for whom they originally were chosen. This decision has since been rescinded; however, for all intents and purposes, candidates maintain control over their delegates with CRA and by virtue of the rules of many of the state parties.

The regular party did try to revivify itself by fiat with the 1982 Hunt Commission reforms. This proved a futile exercise in many respects. One of the main rulings of the Hunt Commission was the reinstitution of winner-take-all types of delegate allocation rules. States were permitted at that time to use either proportional allocation of delegates to the competing presidential candidates or some forms of winner-take-all rules. This change proved unacceptable to delegates at subsequent national conventions and has since been rescinded.

The other major change made by the commission was the creation of so-called superdelegates, a core of ex officio delegates chosen explicitly *not* to be beholden or committed to the candidates. They would come from the ranks of elected officials and from unelected party leadership positions. About half of these superdelegates would not even technically represent states but would be national representatives of the party, free to vote how they pleased at the convention. The total number of superdelegates would make up about 15 percent of the convention delegates.

This reform has never had its intended effect. These superdelegates were supposed to remain uncommitted, and they were expected to lend a representative, deliberative element to the conventions, or at the very least hold sway for the party establishment. Actually, at no convention have the superdelegates played the role envisioned by their creators. Instead, the overwhelming plebiscitary and candidate-centered elements of the campaign have forced the superdelegates' hand. Ironically, this not insubstantial group of nominally uncommitted delegates almost always has pledged support to the active candidates for president rather early in the process. To gain any influence at all they nearly all have seen fit in the campaigns since the Hunt Commission to act as handicappers and commit themselves to a candidate or candidates early on, *often before a single primary has taken place.* As previously noted, party leaders began as early as about 1940 to commit long before the convention because of the candidate-centered type of politics that was developing at the time. The creation of superdelegates was an incredibly naive attempt to bring back a representative type of legitimacy to nomination politics that literally cannot exist in the contemporary political milieu.

The idea that the superdelegates would somehow remain above the fray in the plebiscitary process proved ludicrous. In fact, Paul Kirk, the Democratic national chair during the 1988 race, stated that the candidate with the most delegates coming to the convention should be ratified as the nominee by the convention, regardless of whether he actually had a majority. Presumably the superdelegates would have been encouraged that year by Kirk to throw their weight behind the people's choice in the primaries and caucuses—an odd twist on their intended role of providing careful reflection and reconsideration of the voters' choices for the party—had no candidate actually secured majority support in the primaries.

Although presidential nomination politics already was moving in the direction of more openness and participation and less party control before 1970, the rule changes on the Democratic side were important in codifying and legitimizing the new process. The national party acted forcefully and deliberately to tear control of the state delegations away from party leaders at the state and local levels. The idea of party leaders in the various states acting in the best interest of the rank and file to produce a presidential candidate no longer held sway. In effect, the representative style of legitimacy that once had characterized the Democratic presidential nomination process was gone. It was replaced by legitimacy of the plebiscitary sort. The presidential candidate for the Democrats would be produced by the direct input of the people and be legitimized in that way. Candidate-centered campaigns would characterize nomination politics *because candidates for president and not party leaders* would have control over the delegates at the national convention.

Effects on the Republicans

All of the post-1968 changes in the delegate selection process described above were instituted by the national Democratic party. It is the case, however, that the Republican party has had to live with some of the reforms that the Democrats instituted. In fact, the GOP has, for the most part, been unable or uninterested in resisting the types of changes that were instituted on the Democratic side.

Of course the main trends in the nomination process had nothing to do with the spate of reforms since 1968. The trend of loosened party control over delegates and increasingly candidate-centered politics affected both parties throughout the century irrespective of any institutionalized reforms. And noted earlier, in the case of the Goldwater nomination in 1964, the GOP actually was *more* susceptible than the Democrats to insurgent influence in the process of delegate selection in the states, because of the permeability of the southern state party organizations. But some of the institutionalized Democratic reforms have had some effect on the Republican nomination process. On balance, the Republicans, like the Democrats, now have a nomination process that is dominated by candidate-centered campaigns, with state delegations free from the heavy-handed influence of the regular party leadership.

Of course the mandates of the Democratic reform commissions had no binding effect on the Republican state and local party organizations. The Republican party, in fact, is not in the habit of giving national-level mandates on the state parties as the Democrats are. For example, the GOP has never done away with the unit rule. (The Democrats outlawed it in 1968.) The national Republicans never have required proportional allocation of delegates, nor have they outlawed the winner-take-all primary. The national Republicans do not give the candidates control over their delegates in the same way that the Democrats do with CRA.

However, the process by which the primaries were adopted in so many states after the McGovern-Fraser rule changes did change the GOP delegate selection process. Many Democratically controlled legislatures, when the pressure for reform was coming from the Democratic national party in the early 1970s, instituted presidential primaries for their states that were in many cases to be conducted for both parties. The result was that the number of primaries on the Republican side increased along with the Democrats.

It is important to note that the existence of a primary for a party does not necessarily mean that the primary is the way that delegates will be selected by the party. Traditionally, some states primaries were only a way to poll the rank and file and not necessarily influential in any way in the selection of delegates. The Republicans, while required to hold primaries in many states, did not have to use them for delegate selection as did the Democratic state parties, which were directed by their national party rules. However, most Republican state parties *did* choose to go ahead and use the primaries as their means of selecting and sometimes instructing delegates. Why would they choose to do so?

One reason is that any change in the direction of direct democracy in an era in which direct participatory forms of democracy are so popular is difficult and surely unwise to resist. Mostly, however, Republicans did not even try to buck the trend. In 1972, when the Democrats were holding their open, primary-laden, candidate-centered nomination campaign, the Republicans were renominating a popular incumbent, President Richard Nixon, with only token opposition. When the GOP had a real contest in 1976, the news media and the public already had come to accept and place great emphasis on the primaries—there were more than thirty of them that year. The Republicans had two respected and popular people running for the nomination that year—former Governor Ronald Reagan and President Gerald Ford. There certainly was no reason for the party not to consult and abide by the opinion of the rank and file in choosing its nominee. Most Republican state parties did use primaries to select and instruct their delegations. Plebiscitary democracy came to the Republican presidential nomination process in 1976 without any substantial effort made to resist it.

It bears reemphasis that efforts to resist fully participatory means of delegate selection are manifestly unpopular in this day and age, regardless of party. In 1988, the state parties on the Republican side that resisted opening their delegate selection processes, most notably Michigan and North Carolina, were beset with considerable intraparty dissension, including occasional outbreaks of violence.

The GOP does not have nationally binding rules as the Democrats have. As such, the Republican process has changed less since 1970 than the Democratic process. Note in table 2.3, for example, that more states have voted as a unit on the GOP side. Also, the national Republican party has not required any racial or age quotas in the state delegations. Furthermore, the party has far more variety, including winner-take-all rules, in their methods of delegate allocation. In fact, most state Republican parties use some form of winner-take-all rules in allocating delegates to candidates in primaries and in states with caucus/convention systems.

However, it would be unwise to draw too many significant distinctions between the two parties' processes. Both have primaries and open caucuses that in almost every state determine delegate commitments—commitments made to candidates running nationally for the highest office. Both processes are dominated by independent candidate-centered campaigns. In fact, in the last two nomination races, in 1988 and in 1992, the GOP actually selected *more* of their delegates by primary than the Democrats. In sum, the Republicans have tacitly and without mandate from above gone along with most of the plebiscitary assumptions that were codified by the Democrats after their difficult 1968 convention.

Election Finance Rules and Presidential Nominations

As if the parties were not already in a weakened position vis-à-vis the candidates' independent campaign organizations in nomination politics, Congress passed a landmark law in the 1970s featuring, among other things, the explicit recognition of these campaign organizations. The Federal Election Campaign Act of 1974 (FECA), and subsequent legislation and judicial rulings, further weakened the party leadership in presidential nomination politics.

In the financing of campaigns for all federal offices, the new laws treat political parties as little more than glorified interest groups. Candidates are forced to raise money in relatively small amounts from individuals and groups—no more than $1,000 from individuals and $5,000 from political action committees (PACs). Political parties are treated more or less as though they were PACs; they also are limited to $5,000 direct contributions to candidates. While this restriction does not have much direct impact on presidential nomination races, since many party units around the country do not officially take sides in a nomination fight, the restriction does reduce the potential impact parties can have at all levels of politics.

Parties cannot organize and run all aspects of campaigns for public office with these new restrictions on their financial contributions; hence, they cannot control the politics of their states or localities as they once could. They become, by law, important, but ancillary, players in electoral politics. They can provide support and assistance to candidates running for office (although the amount of support above and beyond direct financial contributions parties can legally offer to candidates also is limited), but they cannot be dominant players. In reality, they are secondary to the campaign apparatuses assembled by the candidates. There are very few places in the country today, if any, in which a candidate can rely on the party organizations to run and win a campaign for office.

Federal election finance laws also actually have enticements of a sort for candidates to run for president. To qualify for the enticements it is necessary for most candidates to set up their campaign organization well in advance (realistically at least a year) of the first primary. Candidates who can raise $5,000 or more in amounts of $250 or less in each of at least twenty states qualify for federal matching funds at regular intervals during the campaign after officially announcing the candidacy. Smaller contributions to the campaign (as well as those meeting the above criteria)—those of $250 or less—henceforth are matched by the federal government.

There are two key ramifications of these laws. One is that the candidate probably will need to set up his campaign apparatus, especially the fund-raising arm of it, quite early in order to develop a geographically broad group of contributors. The other is that, as an aspirant for his or her party's nomination, a candidate must look to individual contributors and the federal government for the support needed to finance a campaign. Money, an indispensable part of any political campaign, does not in large measure come from party connections. The candidate most likely will be dependent on his own organizational ability, and always will be dependent on the federal government, to raise sufficient funds to make a serious run for the party's presidential nomination.

The upshot of the 1974 changes is that *by law* the party takes a backseat to the independent campaign organizations. The new law sped up the trends already affecting nomination politics and made permanent the change. Furthermore, while it is wise and productive for presidential candidates to develop ties to the state and local party organizations while competing for delegates in primaries and caucuses, the fact is that state and local organizations do not control the politics in their area almost anywhere in the country, because candidates for all federal offices are strictly limited in the amount of money they can receive from party organizations. As a result, senators, members of the House, and governors are quite likely to have personal campaign organizations with the ability to organize a state or a district and get out the vote. Presidential candidates are better served in most parts of the country by working through connections with major politicians in a state and not necessarily through the party organization.

Summary

The changes in fund-raising laws for presidential candidates generally are representative of the trends in presidential nomination politics this century. Simply put, candidates for president are free from party control in conducting all the necessary activities to win a presidential nomination, and surely none is more important than raising money.

Candidates cannot wait for a draft at the convention or hope to negotiate a deal in a smoke-filled room to secure the necessary delegates for the nomination. As was noted at the beginning of this chapter, there are three key components to understanding presidential nomination politics. Briefly:

1) A candidate must secure a majority of the delegates at the national convention of his party.
2) The delegates come from fifty state delegations.
3) The state parties determine how to select delegates for the convention, subject to national party rules.

Ever since the Progressive era, the organizational leaders of the parties gradually have had less control over the delegates in their delegations, as well as over the means by which the states select and instruct the delegates. Independent campaign organizations cropped up to compete vigorously for individual delegate and leadership support in the months or even years before the convention. Party leaders quickly learned that the path of withholding support until the convention would not bear fruit, so more and more of them committed early to candidates running national campaigns.

Eventually the push for direct and participatory forms of democracy became irresistible on the Democratic side. A violently tumultuous convention in 1968, brought on in no small measure by an outdated, insufficiently participatory delegate selection process, led to reform. The party codified a plebiscitary, candidate-centered nomination process. The changes in campaign finance laws in 1974 further entrenched this type of nomination process. The Republican party, while not codifying plebiscitary democracy as the Democrats have, has a process nearly indistinguishable from the Democrats' in terms of its open, participatory, and candidate-centered character. The Republicans' inability to resist the changes initiated by Democrats is a testament to the dominance of candidate-centered campaign politics in presidential nomination campaigns.

What has been described in this chapter is the evolution of the presidential nomination process into a procedure for public choice, in principle similar to any single-day election. Candidates compete in an open environment to secure a majority of delegates. While the presidential nomination process is far more complex and convoluted than an ordinary election, it is similar in that the public, through direct participation, determines the winner.

In the past, a representative type of legitimacy characterized presidential nomination politics. This type of process featured intermediation by elite members of the political parties. This elite was empowered by the system to select the nominees for president, or at least to have a considerable impact on the eventual choice. Today, the power in the nomination process over the delegates at the national conventions is held almost exclusively by independent candidate organizations, which compete in a free-for-all to win delegates in public events.

The primary goal of this book is to evaluate the quality of this process of public choice, but first it will look in more detail at the contemporary nomination campaign and the dynamics that influence the outcomes of these campaigns.

Chapter Three

The Current Presidential Nomination Process

This chapter looks in depth at the details, arrangements, and dynamics of contemporary nomination campaigns. Starting with the mechanics of delegate selection. It then goes on to look at the schedule of primaries and precinct caucuses used in the 1992 and 1996 campaigns. Subsequently, the candidates' campaign organizations are described. It focuses particularly on how campaign organizations prepare themselves to compete for delegates during what Arthur Hadley calls the "Invisible Primary," the year or so before delegates actually get selected. It then looks at the dynamics of the campaign during the time when the delegates are selected in primaries and caucuses.

Primaries and Caucuses

As was noted in chapter 2, everything important in presidential nomination campaigns revolves around the selection of delegates who will go to the national convention. These delegates are selected in the states, in ways that the state parties choose, subject to national party rules. There are two ways by which states select, and often instruct, delegates to the parties' quadrennial national nominating conventions. States use either primary elections or a series of party meetings called the caucus/convention system.

Most states—numbering about thirty-five in recent election years—use primaries. Most Americans probably consider these primary elections the fairest or most modern way to go about selecting delegates. Ever since the days of boss-dominated party politics, party meetings have been given a bad name, often associated with heavy-handed undemocratic procedures. But in contemporary U.S. politics, it is better to think of primaries and the caucus/convention system simply as two different styles of participatory democracy, each with its own merits and demerits.

Primaries

Today's presidential primaries resemble the format of the general election. People show up at any time during the day to pick up a ballot and cast a vote for a candidate for president in the privacy of a voting booth. The only real technical difference from participating in a general election is that the list of candidates a particular voter has to choose from are all of the same political party. The voter is choosing among or between candidates of the same party, not between candidates of opposing parties, as is the case in the general election.

In the past, some presidential primaries were quite a bit different from a general election. In some states, no candidates' names would appear on the ballot. Instead, the voter would be confronted with an imposing list of potential delegates. These potential delegates may or may not have had publicly known affiliations with active presidential candidate campaign organizations. To be an informed voter in this environment was quite a task. If one wanted to express a presidential preference in such a primary, one might have had to know a good deal about the potential delegates, most of whom were not well-known public figures.

It was also the case in some states that the primaries were not directly tied to the delegate selection process. They were instead simply *beauty contests.* These primaries were a means by which the organizational party leaders would gauge the sentiments of rank-and-file voters in the party, but they were not used to select delegates.

Today in presidential primaries, in most states, the names of the active candidates for president are listed on the ballot, and in the states in which lists of delegates are on the ballot, it is made clear the active candidacy (if any) associated with the delegates. Some slates of delegates may explicitly be listed as "uncommitted." It is important to note that by participating in primaries the voter actually is voting for delegates, *whether they are listed on the ballot or not.* The key point is that the voter in most cases is voting for delegates who are firmly committed, sometimes by the state party's rules, to one of the candidates. In effect, the voter is directly participating in the selection of a state delegation that likely will be committed to one or more of the active candidates for president.

Primary elections may or may not be open to voters registered as independent or as members of another party. Some states have rules that permit voters to select on primary election day which party's primary they will participate in; in fact, some states do not have registration by party. Other states will permit crossover voting on the primary election day, provided the voter reregisters as a member of the party whose primary he or she is voting in. Other states permit only voters registered in a party to participate in that party's primary. Today most states that hold primaries permit crossover voting or reregistration on the day of the primary election.

Primary outcomes usually are reported in the media just like the outcome of any election. That is, the outcome is reported according to the percentage of the vote that is won by the active candidates involved. It might be something like:

Candidate A received 35 percent of the vote; Candidate B, 25 percent; Candidate C, 18 percent; and so on. But these popular vote results are not exactly, or sometimes even close to, how the delegates who ultimately will represent the state at the national convention will be allocated to the active candidates. The popular vote totals are *not* really what matters in the primaries. What matters is how many delegates from that state the candidate will get in his quest to secure enough delegates to be the presidential nominee. The delegate allotments based on the results in the primary are made in different ways in different states. The two parties' state organizations differ significantly in how they go about allotting delegates.

The Democratic state parties operate under a set of rather restrictive national party rules. The state parties must allot delegates to the candidates based on the outcome of the primaries *proportional to the popular vote totals,* with a few qualifications. First, the proportional allocation may be done based on the outcome of the vote in congressional districts, or by some other subdivision of the state, or it may be done based on the overall statewide vote. Almost every Democratic state party subdivides the state in some way (usually by congressional district) for the purpose of delegate allocation. Second, candidates who get less than 15 percent of the vote are not required to be allocated delegates proportional to their percentage of the popular vote by the state party. In other words, there is in most states a *threshold* of popular votes, under which a candidate is not awarded delegates from his slate to the national convention.

On the Democratic side, therefore, delegate allocation is done in rough proportionality to the percentage of the popular vote secured by the candidate. In a purely proportional system, delegate totals would mirror popular vote outcomes, but since candidates must receive 15 percent of the vote in most states to get *any* delegates, candidates above 15 percent ordinarily receive more delegates than they would win under a purely proportional allocation method.

Republican state parties commonly allot delegates differently from the Democrats. And within the various state party units in the GOP there is far more variation in how delegates get allocated based on primary results. The main reason is that the Republican national party puts no restrictions, such as the national Democrats' proportional requirement, on their state party units.

Republican state parties allocate delegates according to all sorts of rules; many of them have a *winner-take-all* quality to them, as opposed to a proportional quality. Many state parties subdivide into districts and allot all of the delegates in a particular district to the candidate who finishes first in the voting in the district. A couple of states have a pure winner-take-all system in which the first-place finisher statewide gets all of the state's delegates. Some states allot bonus delegates to the candidate who comes in first in the congressional districts. Several states have proportional allocation just like the Democrats require. A few states hold primaries and then decide later in party meetings exactly how to go about allocating the delegates. There also are other hybrid methods combining some of types described above.

Despite the state-by-state variations, some generalizations can be made in comparing the two parties' methods of allocating delegates in the primaries, and the differences are important. The Democrats dictate a form of proportional allocation, which makes it difficult for a single candidate to amass large numbers of delegates as long as several candidates remain active in the race. The reason is that losing candidates in Democratic primaries, provided they surpass the 15 percent threshold, still can accumulate significant delegate support at the convention.

On the other hand, more than half of the Republican state parties do not use the proportional methods of allocation. With many states using winner-take-all types of rules, a leading Republican candidate can control many state delegations, even when several other candidates remain active in the race. Losing candidates tend to accumulate few delegates under winner-take-all types of rules. Thus, a successful Republican candidate for the nomination often is in a position to overwhelm his opponents earlier in the campaign season than his successful counterpart on the Democratic side, who is unable to amass as large a number of delegates under proportional allocation rules.

Caucus/Convention System

About fifteen state parties, both Democratic and Republican, use the caucus/convention system to select delegates to the national convention. The caucus/convention system is, in some respects, a throwback to the days of party-dominated politics. In those days party leaders controlled the caucus and convention meetings, engineering the selection of delegates whom they could control at the national conventions. The caucus/convention method of delegate selection does not operate in that elite-dominated way anymore in almost any state.

The caucus/convention system parallels exactly the way in which parties are organized in the states. In the states, parties have several layers of organization. At the top is the state party, under which are organizational apparatus and officials at the congressional district level, below that are county-level organizations, and at the bottom are precinct organizations. Big cities with large population concentrations often have another level of organization between the precincts and the counties, but it generally is the case, as is laid out below, that parties have four levels of organization in the states: state, congressional district, county, and precinct.

Party Organization at the State Level

State Party
Congressional District
County-Level Organization
Precinct-Level Organization (Caucuses)

All states, usually every two years, have party meetings to discuss matters of policy and organization at all these levels. In some states, in the presidential election year, these party meetings are dominated by presidential politics. About fifteen of the states incorporate the public expression of presidential preference into these party meetings. On the Democratic side, the public expression of presidential preference in the earliest *precinct caucus* round of meetings must be directly linked to the ultimate selection of delegates at the state convention. On the Republican side there is no such hard and fast stipulation, although today all of the GOP state parties permit some form of public expression of presidential preference in the precinct caucuses.

The procedure is as follows: at the earliest and lowest level of party meetings, the precinct caucuses, the public is invited to participate to express a presidential preference by electing representatives of the precinct meeting (these people often have attachments to a candidate's campaign organization) to attend the county-level meeting later in the year. At the county-level meeting, representatives from the open precinct meetings meet and select (usually based on presidential preference in a presidential election year) representatives for the congressional district meeting later in the year. And at the congressional district meeting representatives are selected for the state convention. At the state party convention the actual delegates to the national convention are selected.

This process sounds complicated, but it is, in fact, quite permeable to the ordinary citizen linked up with an active presidential candidacy. If a candidate can get his supporters to infiltrate the precinct caucuses in large numbers, they can elect from among their own to the subsequent party meetings at higher levels and ultimately win most of the delegates from the state to the national convention. Also, some presidential candidacies have, in effect, taken over the state party organizational apparatus as a result of success in these meetings. In recent years, in several states, conservative Christian groups have been energized in presidential election years by candidates (particularly Pat Robertson in 1988) to participate in Republican party meetings. In some of the states where conservative Christians have been most active, this has resulted in an effective takeover of the organizational party by these activists.

These initial precinct caucus meetings are a classic form of grass-roots participatory democracy. People show up at a specific time in the evening at a church, or school, or home. They debate various issues relevant to the members of the party and then, usually openly without secret ballots, vote for the presidential candidate of their choice. Activists linked with the presidential candidates attempt to get selected to attend the next level of meetings at the county level later in the year.

While the results of the polling of the participants at the precinct caucuses ordinarily is what gets reported in the media, the delegates do not actually get selected until the state convention. At that point, circumstances of the presidential race could have changed dramatically, and the candidate who managed successfully to infiltrate the precinct caucuses could long since have dropped out of the race for president. Thus, the candidate commitments of the eventual delegation may not necessarily reflect the outcome of the vote in the precinct caucuses.

Which of these two methods is better, or more fair and democratic? There is no definitive answer to that question. They are two distinctly different forms of participatory democracy. The primaries have the advantage of being simple and secret, but they require very little of the citizen. The caucus/convention system requires active citizen participation in the political process and encourages debate and discussion among participants, but it is less convenient and may be more difficult for many less-educated citizens to participate in a meaningful way.

It certainly is the case that public participation is greater on average in primaries than in caucuses, sometimes dramatically so. Primary participation of eligible voters ranges from 20 to 50 percent in the states, depending a great deal on the sort of media attention given the primary and how hotly contested the primary is by active candidates. Participation in open precinct caucuses almost never exceeds 10 percent of eligible participants and usually is substantially lower. It is important to reemphasize that both are open to public participation, and both allow the public, not party leaders, to determine the makeup of the delegation to the parties' conventions in presidential election years.

The 1992 Race for the Nomination

Table 3.1 has the schedule of primaries and caucuses from the 1992 presidential nomination campaign. Following that, in table 3.2, is the schedule of events for 1996. As can be seen, the events stretch from mid-February into June, with the bulk of the events occurring earlier in that period.

Perhaps the most important development in the scheduling of these events has been the tendency in the last decade or so for states to put primaries and precinct caucuses earlier in the year. This process has been described as "front-loading." If one compares the schedule for 1992 with that for 1996, one can see the changes that have been made in just the last four years. Table 3.3 documents the increasing number of events that are being held early in the campaign. Several larger states have moved up their primaries for the 1996 campaign, as is shown. Much more will be said about front-loading in this and later chapters.

Table 3.1
1992 Schedule of delegate selection events

February 10	Iowa	caucus
February 18	New Hampshire	primary
February 23	Maine	caucus
February 25	South Dakota	primary
March 3	Colorado	primary
	Idaho	caucus (D), primary (R)
	Maryland	primary
	Minnesota	caucus
March 7	Arizona	caucus
	Nevada	caucus
	South Carolina	primary
	Wyoming	caucus
March 10	Delaware	caucus
	Florida	primary
	Georgia	primary
	Hawaii	caucus
	Louisiana	primary
	Massachusetts	primary
	Mississippi	primary
	Missouri	caucus
	Oklahoma	primary
	Rhode Island	primary
	Tennessee	primary
	Texas	primary
March 15	Puerto Rico	primary

Table 3.1—Continued

March 17	Illinois	primary
	Michigan	primary
March 24	Connecticut	primary
March 31	Alaska	caucus
	Vermont	caucus
April 7	Kansas	primary
	New York	primary
	Wisconsin	primary
April 11	Virginia	caucus
April 20	Utah	caucus
April 28	Pennsylvania	primary
May 5	District of Col.	primary
	Indiana	primary
	North Carolina	primary
	Ohio	primary
May 12	Nebraska	primary
	West Virginia	primary
May 19	Oregon	primary
	Washington	primary
May 26	Arkansas	primary
	Kentucky	primary
June 2	Alabama	primary
	California	primary
	Montana	primary
	New Jersey	primary
	New Mexico	primary
June 9	North Dakota	caucus (D), primary (R)

Table 3.2
1996 Schedule of delegate selection events

January 25	Hawaii	caucus (R)
		caucus (D) on March 12
January 26	Alaska	caucus (R)
		caucus (D) on March 9
February 12	Iowa	caucus
February 20	New Hampshire	primary
February 24	Delaware	primary
February 27	Arizona	primary (R)
		primary (D) on March 9
	North Dakota	primary (R)
		caucus (D) on Feb. 29
	South Dakota	primary
March 2	South Carolina	primary
		caucus (D) on March 5
March 3	Puerto Rico	primary (R)
		primary (D) on March 10
March 5	Colorado	primary
	Connecticut	primary
	Georgia	primary
	Idaho	caucus (D)
		caucus (R) on May 28
	Maine	primary
	Maryland	primary
	Massachusetts	primary
	Minnesota	caucus
	Rhode Island	primary
	Vermont	primary
March 7	New York	primary
	Missouri	caucus (D)
		caucus (R) on March 9
March 10	Nevada	caucus
March 12	Florida	primary
	Louisiana	primary

	Mississippi	primary

Table 3.2—Continued

	Oklahoma	primary
	Oregon	primary
	Tennessee	primary
	Texas	primary
March 16	Michigan	primary (D)
		primary (R) on March 19
March 19	Illinois	primary
	Ohio	primary
	Wisconsin	primary
March 23	Wyoming	caucus
March 25	Utah	caucus
March 26	California	primary
	Washington	caucus
April 2	Kansas	primary
April 13	Virginia	caucus
April 23	Pennsylvania	primary
May 7	District of Col.	primary
	Indiana	primary
	North Carolina	primary
May 14	Nebraska	primary
	West Virginia	primary
May 21	Arkansas	primary
May 28	Kentucky	primary
June 4	Alabama	primary
	Montana	primary
	New Jersey	primary
	New Mexico	primary

Table 3.3
Front-loading delegate selection events

A. *The Progression of Front-loading*

Number of states holding primaries or precinct caucuses by March 31 (including District of Columbia and Puerto Rico)

1980	19
1984	29
1988	30
1992	30
1996	38

Number of states holding primaries or precinct caucuses by March 14 (including District of Columbia and Puerto Rico)

1980	15
1984	15
1988	22
1992	24
1996	30

B. *Percentage of Delegates Selected, 1992 and 1996*

	Democrats	
	March 14	March 31
1992	34.7	45.4
1996	49.0	76.4

	Republicans	
	March 14	March 31
1992	37.0	42.5
1996	49.6	74.7

The Invisible Primary

When the participatory, primary-dominated nomination process still was relatively new in the mid-1970s, Arthur Hadley wrote a book entitled *The Invisible Primary*. He claims in this book that the most important events in presidential nomination campaigns occurs before a single state actually holds its primary. He believes that the informed observer could make an intelligent guess as to which candidate would get a party's nomination by rating the candidates on what they did in the year or more before the Iowa precinct caucuses and the New Hampshire primary kicked off the delegate selection season.

Hadley's thesis is an implicit recognition of the centrality of candidate-centered campaign organizations in modern presidential nomination politics. Predicting the outcome, he is saying in effect, is a matter of the quality of the candidates' campaign organizations, which a keen observer was in a position to judge before Iowa or New Hampshire. (The book, which is completed about January 1976, did a remarkable job of anticipating which candidates were prepared on the Democratic side to make a serious run for the nomination that year.) Certainly anticipating the outcome or handicapping the race has little to do with what the *parties* as organizational units are doing.

Hadley is right. A candidate cannot possibly do well in the grueling schedule of events in the three and a half months of caucuses and primaries without laying the groundwork with a sophisticated campaign organization. In fact if one identifies the right factors, one can assess which candidates are in a position to do well once the delegates actually are selected.

Borrowing from Hadley's list of six key factors in the invisible primary, as well as from journalistic and scholarly accounts and analyses of the last several campaigns, there appear to be three essential ingredients for success in the earliest stages of a presidential campaign.

1. Single-Mindedness
2. Money
3. Staff and Strategy

Single-Mindedness

Everything important (and certainly the other key ingredients) in a presidential nomination campaign necessarily follows from the single-minded focus of the candidate on winning the presidential nomination. The sort of commitment involved in making a campaign organization competitive requires the full-time effort of the candidate.

A candidate for president depends on the efforts of dozens and even hundreds of workers, some paid and some volunteer, and these workers need to be the sort willing to work twelve or sixteen hours a day for the cause. The candidate who cannot himself put in that kind of effort has a great deal of difficulty inspiring the efforts of the staff and volunteers. Only the rare candidate, who has a particularly inspiring message and motivated supporters, can afford not to make the same sort of personal commitment to the campaign as the workers must. Ronald Reagan was such a candidate in 1980. His schedule was notably relaxed compared to most of his competitors, or to anyone running for president in recent years. Of course, he did have the rare ability to inspire herculean efforts on the part of legions of staff and volunteers without running himself ragged. But most candidates for president do not have the sort of charisma and inspiring message that Reagan did, and they must motivate their supporters based in large measure on their own desire to put in the effort required.

The reality of the modern campaign is such that simply raising enough money to continue week by week requires an unusual level of perseverance. Above and beyond that, following through on a winnable campaign strategy forces a candidate to make speeches and appearances at a breakneck pace for months. The typical candidate for president is not a nationally known figure, either among the general public or even sometimes among the politically attentive around the country. Rallying support, winning over potential campaign workers, keeping the campaign together through the inevitable pitfalls of a hotly competitive political race, and developing some mastery over the details of issues affecting the people you will meet all around the country is more than a full-time job. The energy, commitment, and devotion to do these things, *and* raise money, require a superhuman effort on the part of the candidate. Any ambivalence about running, any need for vacation time, and certainly the need to fulfill work obligations that are more than perfunctory, almost certainly will doom any candidacy. Richard Ben Cramer recently wrote a detailed account of "What It Takes" to run for president in the U.S. political context. His account of the campaign of Senator Robert Dole in 1988 is particularly telling. The rigors and demands of the race wore down the Senate leader, and he never was willing to undertake the kind of personal effort required to get the Republican nomination.

Money

Even a candidate with the necessary single-minded focus on winning the presidential nomination cannot go far without money. After the commitment to winning, everything about the nuts and bolts of running the campaign and competing for delegates follows from fund-raising. Simply put, it is possible to *buy* the expertise to devise a competitive campaign.

It is hard to quarrel with the contention that money is the most important variable in winning a nomination campaign. In fact, since 1980 the candidate with the most money in the bank going into the Iowa caucuses—that is, before a single delegate had been selected—has been the nominee of his party every time. Having the most money did not guarantee the nomination of Ronald Reagan and Jimmy Carter in 1980, Walter Mondale in 1984, Michael Dukakis and George Bush in 1988, and Bill Clinton and George Bush in 1992. After all, both Jimmy Carter in 1976 and George McGovern in 1972, the eventual nominees, were outspent by a couple of their rivals. A candidate, however, absolutely must have *enough* money to compete effectively and be a viable candidate.

The primaries happen too fast and are too costly for someone to come into the first event with little or no money in reserve and hope to parlay a good showing in Iowa into a successful national campaign. In 1996, candidates probably will need to have somewhere in the neighborhood of ten million dollars in the bank (and maybe much more) heading into the first events if they are to have any hope of being able successfully to compete in subsequent weeks in the southeast, in California, and in the midwest.

So where does all this money come from? As noted in chapter 2, some of the money can come from the federal government. But the candidate must raise a great deal on his own before the federal matching funds amount to much. There is, in effect, within the campaign a campaign to raise money that is every bit as competitive, and every bit as important, as the campaign for delegates in February to June of the election year.

The Wall Street Journal (Special Report: December 4, 1987) distilled the fund-raising component of the modern nomination campaign to "six rules of the game."

Rule #1, Find some fat cats, quick

The reason for the primacy of some big early money is that starting a presidential campaign is like starting any large enterprise. There is a critical need for a large sum of money to get off the ground. Office space has to be rented, consultants and staff have to be hired, polling needs to be undertaken, and many other things. These all cost a great deal of money, but current law outlaws large contributions from any one source, so candidates have to tap into networks of wealthy donors. (The Bush campaign in 1988 is a perfect example. They broke all the records up to that time by tapping into a network of donors that, by the end of the primaries, produced 17,000 people who gave the maximum $1,000 contribution.) Luckily there are consultants who specialize in identifying wealthy donors—but there is a catch—these consultants cost big money, too!

Rule #2, Go where the money is

Each party has its own regular sources of campaign funds that, while extensive, are at the same time limited. The year or two before the election features regular stops on the campaign trail at fund-raising functions, most of them private affairs. So candidates, sometimes alone and sometimes in groups, are invited to speak before influential groups of businesspeople and other likely donors, so the donors can get a firsthand look at the candidates.

On the Democratic side, the large sums of money are likely to come out of the liberal financial elite in New York City and the entertainment establishment in California. Moderate Democrats also may compete for money among the banking and insurance establishment in the South, much of which still is Democratic (a vestige of the "Solid Democratic South" of decades past), or at least maintains ties with prominent Democrats. (It is possible, however, that the 1994 congressional realignment in this region may have affected the allegiances of some of the relevant donors. The next competitive Democratic nomination campaign may prove less hospitable to moderate Democratic candidates as they try to raise campaign funds.)

For example, in the 1988 campaign (which started in earnest in 1987), many observers felt that the real battle among liberal contenders Gary Hart, Joseph Biden, and Michael Dukakis took place in fund-raisers in Los Angeles and New York. Gary Hart initially was winning the battle in 1987, until his campaign foundered on a sex scandal. This left Dukakis and Biden to compete for the available "liberal money," a competition Dukakis ultimately won in a battle of attrition that eventually forced Biden to drop out because of a different sort of scandal.

In the GOP, the competition centers around fund-raisers involving Sunbelt industrialists in oil, textiles, and other industries, and among the Republican-leaning financial elite in New York and other large cities around the country. Direct mail solicitation of conservatives and the religious right also is a hotly competitive area for Republican fund-raising. Millions of dollars can be had with the right pitch to a good mailing list, as Oliver North found in his unsuccessful bid for a Virginia Senate seat in 1994.

Surely the tone of the 1996 GOP race will be set on the basis of which of the myriad of conservative candidates likely to run does best in fund-raisers in the Sunbelt in 1995, as well as in direct mail solicitation.

Rule #3, Tap federal subsidies

As described in chapter 2, donations up to $250 from individuals are matched by the federal government. There are strings attached, however. In accepting federal money, candidates must agree to abide by spending limits, both for individual state events and for the campaign as a whole. But candidates are willing to live by these limits for a couple of reasons.

First, a campaign can operate in the red for extended periods of time knowing that it has qualified for future federal matching dollars based on donations to date. Also, presidential campaigns do not have to worry as much as campaigns for other offices about the efficiency of their fund-raising techniques. This is particularly true in the area of direct mail solicitation of money. Direct mail solicitation, if done inefficiently, may cost a campaign about as much money to conduct as can be raised. This seems not to be a productive way to go about financing a campaign. But in presidential nomination politics, even if it costs one dollar to raise each dollar for your campaign, the trade-off is worth it because the government will match much of the money that is raised.

Rule #4, Flash a big roll

During the long invisible primary, reporters have little to go on in handicapping the race. One of the few concrete signs of success is how much money each candidate has. This can be absolutely critical to a candidate as he tries to establish his viability for a number of reasons. A sort of snowball effect can take place. A "big roll" can lead to more publicity in the news media, increasing a candidate's perceived viability for the nomination, thereby enhancing his ability to raise still more money.

Rule #5, Get used to bureaucracy

The rules for fund-raising are so stringent and complex that an entire bureaucracy is needed in each campaign organization just to ensure compliance with the federal guidelines. Violations of federal fund-raising laws are commonplace, and can incur heavy fines. Applications for matching funds are extremely cumbersome and require copious information about each of the donors. Campaigns need to be scrupulous to avoid large penalties that come with infractions of the rules.

Rule #6, Cheat

Once a candidate accepts the matching money from the government, the state-by-state limits take effect. The limits on spending in some of the smaller important states, such as Iowa and New Hampshire, can be a real nuisance. Money spent on advertising for New Hampshire emanating from Boston television stations can legitimately be put on the Massachusetts account. But many campaigns over the years have been cited for putting on the account of one state expenditures that actually were made in another state. Walter Mondale's 1984 presidential campaign spent nearly *seven times* the legal limit in New Hampshire. While the penalties for such a violation can be fairly stiff, they did not affect the Mondale campaign politically, nor have they ever actually been politically damaging, because they often are assessed long after the violation has occurred. (Mondale, in spite of the excessive expenditures made in the state, lost the primary to a candidate who stayed within the legal limits.)

The viability of presidential campaigns is likely to be determined in the fund-raising phase of the competition. Again, money itself does not win the nomination, but to emerge as a serious contender during the primaries, a candidate needs large sums of money in the bank.

Staff and Strategy

Assuming that a candidate has the drive and single-mindedness, as well as the money, the campaign becomes a matter of what the candidate does with it. Essentially, drive and cash are the raw materials of a successful nomination campaign. The question is: What do you make out of that raw material? What a campaign needs is a competent and organized staff and a sound strategy for securing the nomination. The candidate himself also must have the discipline to carry out the strategy.

Staffing a presidential campaign is no easy task, as one might expect. There are a limited number of people in either party who have experience running a successful presidential campaign. These presidential-campaign-tested campaign experts, usually referred to as *consultants,* become very hot property. Of nearly equal importance to the contest for money sources is the contest to sign up these experienced winners in nomination campaigns. They are in especially short supply because many of the better ones sit out the primaries until there is a nominee, and then they sign up for the general election campaign, where the money is better.

The consultants' view often is that *any* candidacy, of the several that usually are in the running, is a long shot. Most candidates have trouble raising money— hence the decision by many of the best consultants to sit out the uncertain invisible primary and delegate selection process in the primaries and caucuses. In lieu of consultants with experience in presidential campaigns, consultants with recent successes in prominent senate and gubernatorial races are sought after. A famous recent example is that of James Carville, whose dramatic success in a Pennsylvania special Senate election made him hot property on the Democratic side. He signed on with the presidential campaign of Governor Bill Clinton, which propelled Carville to the national prominence he now enjoys.

A presidential campaign needs experts in fund-raising, polling, advertising, organizational issues, and strategy formation. Entire firms are hired to take on these tasks and to coordinate them. It is literally impossible for the candidate to keep track of and control all aspects of the campaign. As a result, the candidate also benefits from having a personal staff with some experience in national politics that is, above all, loyal to him to look out for his interests in the formation of the campaign and its strategy. Remember that the consultants hired to do the technical tasks of a modern campaign often have not had any long-term relationship with the candidate. It is absolutely necessary for the candidate to put together a personal staff that can manage successfully and work well with the professional campaign operatives.

The essence of a successful strategy is to have a plan—a "how to"—for winning the nomination. The campaign must have identified the sorts of voters that are needed to win a sufficient number of delegates in the primaries and caucuses, it must figure out a way to appeal successfully to them, and it must set up the organizational staff around the country to carry out the plan. The candidate is, of course, ultimately responsible for the plan, and *especially is responsible for sticking to it.*

Most candidates for president are not well enough known to have a reliable base of support to build on in the campaign. Candidates who were nationally prominent before the campaign, such as Ronald Reagan, Jesse Jackson, or Pat Robertson, are exceptions. Without a reliable base, most start from scratch in identifying the voters to go after, crafting a message and a method to get their support, and setting up the nuts-and-bolts organization to carry out the plan. Carrying all this out in the modern media-dominated campaign environment is a sophisticated, technical, and highly uncertain undertaking. In fact, most serious candidates for president find themselves struggling to find the right message and tone right up to the first events in February. Sometimes there are dramatic shifts in the focus and strategy of the campaign long after it has been under way. These usually are signs of desperation that indicate a flagging effort. But occasionally these shifts are successful. In the case of Gary Hart in 1984, a remaking of the message shortly before the Iowa caucuses put him in serious contention for the nomination. His "new ideas" made him the viable alternative to front-runner Mondale. Also, Dick Gephardt in 1988 changed the tone of his message shortly before Iowa; this shift worked to propel him to a come-from-behind victory there.

Campaign technology has all the appearance of a science but it is a highly experimental and inexact one at best and probably is better thought of as an art form. Even so, there clearly are better and worse practitioners of the art, and retaining or finding the better ones is one of the keys to a successful nomination campaign.

Who Can Compete?

Given the above requirements for the development of a successful campaign, what sorts of people are likely to be able to compete?

It is impossible to define specifically the qualities of a successful presidential candidate. After all, the nominees in recent years have come from all kinds of backgrounds. Governors, retired governors, a senator, vice presidents, and former vice presidents all have been successful candidates for their party's presidential nomination. Former senators, a former House member, and others have emerged as serious contenders. But there are some generalizations that can be made about the type of people who can become major contenders.

Naturally, the serious contender has to be fully committed to running for president. He has to be in a position to spend his or her full time campaigning and raising money. Congressman Morris Udall once said that the presidency today is reserved for the unemployed and those willing to shirk their present duties. There is more than a kernel of truth in that statement. Presidents Carter and Reagan, as well as Vice President Walter Mondale, were not holding any office when they succeeded in winning their party's nomination. Many contenders from Congress have had to make the decision whether to show up for important votes and committee meetings or make a serious run for the presidency.

For example, Senator Robert Dole and Congressman Richard Gephardt both had to decide whether to keep up with their duties in Congress when running for president in 1988. Dole remained active in Washington, Gephardt did not. While neither, of course, succeeded in securing his party's nomination, in Gephardt's case it certainly was not because of any lack of commitment to the race; his personal commitment involved moving his entire family into an apartment in Iowa for several months in the year preceding the caucuses. In Dole's case, his decision to retain an active interest in his duties as minority leader of the Senate probably was a significant factor in his failure to receive the Republican presidential nomination.

Dole's main rival that year, Vice President Bush, while not unemployed, certainly benefited from the flexibility of his job. Vice presidents have only one constitutionally required duty, to preside over the Senate, which they ordinarily abdicate almost all the time, whether or not they happen to be running for president. Vice presidents are in a uniquely advantageous position to campaign full-time while still holding public office.

Sitting governors have been successful on the Democratic side in each of the last two campaigns. This fact seems to go against the general rule of needing the time and flexibility to commit fully to the campaign, since governors, unlike senators or members of the House, are executives primarily responsible for the performance of their branch of government in their states. Governor Mario Cuomo of New York regularly has claimed not to be able to commit to the rigors of the presidential campaign while still attending to his state's budget and other matters.

So how did Governors Dukakis and Clinton succeed? In Clinton's case, a capacity to function with little sleep and his prodigious energy, and perhaps some shirking of gubernatorial responsibility, permitted him to commit fully to the campaign trail. In Dukakis's case, a similar energy level and the wise use of his time back home to national political advantage, by arranging for the media to be there to report his conscientious attention to duty, allowed for some balance between duty and campaign commitment. (It should be noted that the mania of the presidential race was not without cost to Dukakis's family life after the campaign.)

There is, however, a particular advantage to being a sitting governor, such as Dukakis and Clinton, that can work partially to offset whatever disadvantage the requirements of governing a state can have. Governors are in a position to raise a tremendous amount of money from business interests regulated in any way by the state. Businesses, whether fervent supporters or not, are more than happy to contribute to the campaign of the governor, because of the potential political power wielded by the governor over contracts or any of the regulatory apparatus of the state.

Members of Congress on influential committees are similarly situated to raise large amounts of money from the interests that are potentially regulated or taxed by the committee. Also, any candidate with a built-in national following can tap this source of campaign funds through direct mail.

Senators and governors can be at an advantage in the area of staff as well. Both have, with their office, a large personal staff that can be instrumental in running the complex enterprise of a presidential campaign. Remember that while candidates must hire the specialized skills of consultants, they may not have long-term personal connections with and trust in the hired expert help. An experienced personal staff can provide the necessary control over the workings of the campaign to bridge successfully the interests of the candidate and the operations of the political consultants.

To summarize, the contemporary campaign context favors any candidate in a position to commit his time fully to the campaign. Prominent former officeholders are at an advantage, but those in office who are willing or able to step away from their duties for the year or so prior to the Iowa caucuses also can compete. Congressmen heading up powerful committees, governors, and people with a national following have an advantage in fund-raising. Senators and governors also have some marginal advantage because of the large staffs they have at their disposal.

All of the effort in setting up a campaign in the invisible primary is aimed, of course, at the primaries and caucuses starting in February of the election year. It is here that delegates actually are won. For all of the preparation for these events, rarely do candidacies last the entire schedule of primaries and caucuses. In fact, it is rare that more than two candidates still are actively competing for delegates all the way through the primary season. Most candidates for president either drop out of the race altogether, freeing their delegates to choose among the remaining contenders, or suspend their campaigns, but retain control over the delegates they have won thus far. These dynamics of the modern campaign are the subject of the next section.

"Big MO"—The Dynamics of Presidential Nomination Campaigns

With the frequently large fields of active candidates, it is a wonder that any one candidate can amass a majority of the delegates nationwide during the primaries. Some candidates are casualties of the so-called invisible primary, but many last to compete in the early caucuses and primaries. The following is a list of the number of active candidates contesting the first events in all of the contested nomination races since 1972.

	Democratic candidates	Republican candidates
1972	4	uncontested
1976	8	2
1980	2	6
1984	7	uncontested
1988	7	5
1992	5	2

In spite of the large multicandidate fields in most of the contested races, no convention went beyond the first ballot, and only one convention did not have a clear front-runner heading into the balloting. The front-runner emerged in all cases based on delegates won in mostly open competition in primaries and caucus/convention states. Ironically, the convention that was still up in the air was the 1976 Republican convention that featured only two candidates, Reagan and Ford, who were so close in delegates coming in that a very small number of uncommitted delegates held sway.

Inexorably, it seems, the field of candidates is pared down to the point that one candidate is in a position to secure a majority of the delegates during the public events leading up to the convention. John Aldrich (1980) was one of the first to notice the winnowing effect of the *serialization* of presidential primaries—that is, that they occur in sequence over the course of a few months. The dynamics of the process of presidential primaries, he wrote, tend to force candidates out of the race as a function of a variety of factors. These factors include a decreasing likelihood of winning the nomination, a failure to meet performance expectations generally understood to apply to the candidate, a dearth of delegates won by the candidate, and dwindling financial resources. Aldrich found that the more candidates who enter a race, the faster those who fail to do well fall by the wayside in favor of those who can generate some positive momentum with strong early performances.

A slightly different, but not incompatible, angle on the question of the dynamics of presidential nomination campaigns, is taken by Steven Brams (1978). He notes the phenomenon of the weeding out of what are, in effect, trial-balloon candidacies. He notes that each of the ideological perspectives in a party cannot very long sustain more than one candidate. And if more than two perspectives within a party produce candidates, the one in the middle of a left-right ideological spectrum gets squeezed out. It is therefore likely that no more than two candidates will remain viable throughout the race. Paul Gurian (1986) adds that candidates who do poorly invariably suffer from media inattention and an inability to continue to raise money.

The relevant effect of these generally accepted dynamics is that most of the candidates drop out or are forced out after only a small portion of the delegates are selected. The weeding out process really is quite ruthless. The upshot is that the best positioned of the few surviving candidates is in a position to accumulate a majority of delegate support for the national convention.

The schedule of events in tables 3.1 and 3.2 give a more concrete sense of the typical process of attrition in a presidential nomination campaign. Since 1984 there has been a large multistate event held in early March, dominated by southern states. Even that early many of the candidates are in no position to compete seriously for a lion's share of the delegates at stake that day. It is a costly proposition to advertise in these states, and few of the candidates can afford it, even that early in the race. The following chart indicates the number of candidates in each of the last three election years who were in a position financially to compete for large numbers of the delegates up for grabs on the so-called Super Tuesday event:

	Democratic candidates	Republican candidates
1984	4 (Hart, Jackson, Mondale, John Glenn—although Glenn was substantially weakened)	uncontested

	Democratic candidates	Republican candidates
1988	3 (Al Gore, Jackson, and Dukakis—and Paul Simon tried unsuccessfully to reignite his campaign later)	2 (Bush, Dole— Robertson still hanging on, barely)
1992	3 (Clinton, Jerry Brown and Paul Tsongas— although the latter two were unable to compete for large numbers of delegates)	1 (Bush—although Buchanan competed in selected states)

The shakedown of candidates in these races was rather quick, achieved largely on the basis of success or failure in a few early states. Let us take a closer look at *when* and *why* so many of these candidates dropped out so early in these recent races.

1984   Democrats
George McGovern: The McGovern campaign never raised much money. It performed poorly in Iowa but reasonably well in New Hampshire, surprising many experts. Still, the New Hampshire performance was overshadowed by Gary Hart's astounding victory, and McGovern was in no position to compete in several states on one day, particularly in a region of the country inhospitable to his views.
Ernest Hollings: Hollings's showing was so poor in the first two events (Iowa and New Hampshire) that he was unable to compete in his home area of the south. Hollings was low on money, and the weak efforts in the north caused the media largely to ignore his candidacy in favor of the front-runners.
Alan Cranston: Cranston's single-note theme of "nuclear freeze" did not resonate in the first two states. He had no money and no potential constituency in the south.
John Glenn: Glenn did compete for delegates in the south, and still had some money left, but he was in a weakened position. His status as national hero gave him a core of support in these states, but he had fallen woefully short of the high expectations people had for him in the first two states, given his stature. The media darling was Gary Hart; Jesse Jackson had a firmer base in the region, as did Mondale, who also had far more money.

1988 Democrats
Paul Simon: Simon had failed to win Iowa, a neighboring state to his home state of Illinois, and his campaign never really recovered. Money was getting short, and Simon had no potential base in the south.
Gary Hart: Hart had been mortally wounded by adultery charges long before even Iowa. But he reentered the early states, did poorly, and could not compete for large numbers of delegates anywhere, and certainly not on Super Tuesday.
Richard Gephardt: Gephardt won Iowa, a momentum booster, but came in a distant second to Dukakis in New Hampshire. Still, his candidacy was more successful heading into the south than any other, with the possible exception of Dukakis's. Further in his favor was his reputation as a moderate border state representative. The south could have been fertile ground for him, but financial shortfalls left him unable to challenge Gore for moderate white southern votes across the region.
Bruce Babbitt: Babbitt's poor showing in Iowa and lack of money left him unable to campaign widely in New Hampshire, much less on Super Tuesday.

1988 Republicans
Alexander Haig: Haig did very poorly in Iowa and was unable to gain attention or financial support for New Hampshire. He had dropped out well before Super Tuesday.
Jack Kemp: Kemp failed to meet high expectations in the first two states, having finished far behind Bush, Robertson, and Dole in Iowa, and Bush and Dole in New Hampshire. His campaign also was running low on cash. He could not compete seriously for delegates across a broad region.
Pierre DuPont: DuPont's unorthodox message did not go over well in either of the first two states. The financial barrier was potentially surmountable, but DuPont would have received little press attention in the south as a result of his extremely weak early finishes.
Pat Robertson: Robertson did continue to campaign in parts of the south, but he was unable to capitalize in New Hampshire on his strong Iowa showing and rapidly was being consigned to the second tier of candidates by the media.

1992 Democrats
Tom Harkin: Harkin was unable to win outside of his home state of Iowa, losing a critical early battle to Kerrey in neighboring South Dakota. That, together with his losses in South Carolina and New Hampshire, forced him to drop out, largely for financial reasons.
Bob Kerrey: Kerrey also refused to go further into debt, after failing to win anywhere other than in neighboring South Dakota. He proved unable to beat Clinton in the earlier Georgia primary and could not compete effectively on Super Tuesday.

1992 Republicans

Pat Buchanan: Despite surprisingly good showings in New Hampshire and Georgia against President Bush, Buchanan never got a victory or much money. He was in no position at any time to compete for large numbers of delegates.

There are two common denominators in these races: money and media attention. Both are tied to the level of early success a candidate has. A failure to win early, coupled with no money in the bank, makes continuing a race for the nomination next to impossible. The only way to avoid throwing in the towel is if the campaign has raised enough money to pay for its own publicity. This is the only way a campaign can battle the early consignment to second-tier status that results from a loss that leads to lack of coverage from the national and local media.

The fact is that very few presidential candidates go into Iowa and New Hampshire with large cash reserves on hand. The invisible primary is expensive, and most candidates depend on early victories to get them more contributions and the media attention they need when they campaign around the country. The only candidate in recent years to avoid that predicament has been Jesse Jackson, who without cash reserves or early victories has gone on to compete successfully in later states and was Dukakis's only surviving viable challenger through much of the 1988 race. But Jackson has two qualities most politicians do not have. He has a large built-in constituency of blacks and white liberal activist supporters, and he is a famous and attractive draw for media markets of almost any size.

In summary, there are two ways to remain a viable competitor past the early primaries and caucuses: have lots of money on hand or win early to generate publicity and new contributions. In 1984, 1988, and 1992, only a few candidates met the first qualification. In 1984, only Mondale and Glenn had enough money to compete much further than Iowa and New Hampshire without a victory to generate publicity. Hart got the big victory to keep his campaign afloat. In 1988, only Dukakis had big money on the Democratic side; in the GOP, Dole and Bush had enough on reserve to continue to compete past the early events. In 1992, the only candidates on either side with solid financial backing were President Bush and Clinton.

Expectations and Momentum

Political scientist Larry Bartels (1988) has produced the most comprehensive study of the anatomy of momentum for presidential candidates. Putting the 1984 Democratic race under the microscope, he explains how and why voters rallied behind Senator Gary Hart as he emerged from unknown status to national renown as a viable contender for the nomination.

Hart surprised insiders in the media and in Democratic politics by coming in second (actually a distant second) to Walter Mondale, and ahead of the better-known John Glenn, in the Iowa precinct caucuses. The attendant publicity allowed Hart to overtake Mondale in the polls in New Hampshire in just a few days, and emerge victorious in that state by a comfortable margin. Most New

Hampshirans had heard of Gary Hart only for a matter of a week or two, but a sizable plurality was willing to support him on primary day.

In fact, Bartels shows that many Democrats could not really place Hart's positions on the issues of the day or accurately describe his ideological orientation at this early stage in the race for delegates. More or less across the ideological spectrum in the Democratic party, voters were lining up to support this fresh new face. Apparently the surge in his support in New Hampshire, as well as around the country, was a reuslt of his *not being Mondale.* He had emerged as an attractive alternative to the putative front-runner, so the anti-Mondale vote coalesced around him, at least for a time.

In some respects, voters were supporting Hart, not because of the issues, but *because he was winning.* The expectations that voters had about his chances for success helped to build momentum for him. Some form of a political bandwagon seemed to form, based on the success he was having and his status as *the* viable alternative to the front-runner. Hart was (any little-known candidate is) a blank slate to voters. This was to his advantage, as he gained the early support of people who, if they had known more about him, might not have supported him!

Bartels carefully documented how voters across the country, given several weeks to digest the information available about this newly prominent candidate, were able to assess him reasonably accurately in terms of his issue positions and ideological orientation. Consequently, voters increasingly began to link their choice with the issue positions, and Hart's support began to erode. In effect, voters *learned* a great deal about the candidate, given the time to digest the available information about him. In the meantime, however, Hart had the opportunity to capitalize on his surprise early showings to gather support before the dust had settled and voters had the opportunity soberly to assess his qualifications.

The evidence presented by Bartels and many others strongly suggests that the media coverage of the primaries focuses on "the horserace," that is, who is winning and who is losing, particularly early in the delegate selection season. A fresh face garners positive publicity for a time based simply on his good showings, before voters are exposed to more substantive information about issue positions, character, and so forth.

This is the essence of momentum—gaining support that may not otherwise be yours or be likely to stay with you for the long haul of the campaign. It is most important to note that such momentum can have a tremendous impact on a nomination race. The coalescing of support around a seemingly attractive and successful alternative to a front-runner (like Hart was to Mondale) forces many of the other candidates to the sidelines because of the inexorable winnowing process. Candidates like Hart become the reasonable alternative to the front-runner and may survive the primaries and, if things go particularly well, become the nominee.

Most candidates do not have Hart's good fortune to have become a viable contender. The opposite sort of momentum is a downward spiral that affects most of the candidates. Instead of gathering support from people jumping on the bandwagon because of positive publicity, most candidates lose potential support because of their inability to keep their names prominent in the race. Early losses for most candidates lead to less media attention and an inability to raise more money. The candidate falls off the radar screen because he or she loses free media attention and cannot pay for the advertising necessary to stay on the radar screen of the average voter.

Bartels developed a "Typology of Primary Campaigns" (1988, 166-71) that helps us to understand the workings of the complex dynamics of presidential nomination races and to put together the pieces of how momentum works. Contested nomination campaigns fit into one of three types.

1. *Two Major Candidates:* This is when two well-known major figures with established constituencies compete for a nomination. The Reagan-Ford battle in 1976 and the Carter-Kennedy contest in 1980 fit this type.

2. *One Major Candidate:* A clear front-runner exists in many of the races. In 1980 Reagan was the clear front-runner for the GOP, in 1984 Mondale was for the Democrats, and in 1988 Bush was the clear front-runner in his party.

3. *No Major Candidates:* Several candidates competing, but there is no clear favorite, because none is wellknown. There was no front-runner for the Democrats in 1976, 1988, and 1992.

In the first type, candidates are well known and have established bases of support. Momentum is not likely to play a large role, according to Bartels, because voters already know where the candidates stand and are likely to support one of the candidates on that basis and not based on how well he is doing. These races resemble pitched battles in which the candidates do everything they can to rally their supporters, identify the few undecided voters, and get the vote out among their constituencies.

In the second type, there usually is some substantial opposition to the front-runner, as there was to Reagan in 1980, Mondale in 1984, and Bush in 1988. The dynamics of the process dictate that only one of the little-known candidates will emerge as the reasonable alternative to the front-runner. This happens for a couple of reasons. One is that most of the candidates will not have the money to continue once they lose early—only so many candidates can do well in the Iowa and New Hampshire events. The other is that the emerging alternative, because he often is a blank slate given his lack of previous notoriety, can gather surprising momentum and support early, some from voters attracted to his early successes (a kind of bandwagon) and some because voters opposing the front-runner deem him the viable alternative. It could be that candidates Hart and Bush in 1980 lasted as an alternative to the front-runner for such a long time because they were so little known at the time and thus were able to expand their bases of support, while Dole in 1988 was too well known and fixed in voters' minds and was unable to last as an alternative to front-runner Bush that year. In these campaigns the interesting battle is among the lesser-known candidates, to see which one will emerge as the viable alternative to the front-runner for the party's nomination.

In the third type of campaign, with no major candidates, the campaign resembles a free-for-all. All the candidates try desperately to define themselves in a way appealing to their party's voters. The candidates know that they must win early to avoid the downward spiral of financial insolvency and media inattention that afflicts most campaigns. (Candidates in these sorts of campaigns rarely have the resources to survive without free media.) In this type of campaign, therefore, the candidates trot out various gimmicks and slogans to try to separate themselves from the pack. Their reputations and ideologies are not fixed in voters' minds, so there is more freedom to define and redefine themselves to reach into various of the constituencies in the parties. Still, as with the other types, two or three candidates are likely to emerge, and voters, as the campaign progresses, will learn more about the candidates and be in a position to be better able to place them ideologically. It is critical for a candidate to gather momentum and eliminate rivals early before his or her reputation gets fixed.

Conclusion

This chapter has looked at the nuts and bolts of contemporary nomination campaigns, from the workings of the primaries and caucuses to the setting up of campaign organizations, as well as at the complex dynamics of the delegate selection process. These are the essential features of this peculiar, distinctive, and important method of public choice.

Building on this understanding of the contemporary nomination process, Chapter 4 will evaluate its quality as a method of public choice, laying out the thinking and the debates. It also will take a look at some of the proposals for reform of the process that have generated interest in the past twenty-five years.

Chapter Four

Reforming the System?

The presidential nomination process probably has generated as much controversy in the last twenty years as any other single aspect of the political system. There is an interesting confluence of trends and events that helps explain why the nomination process has become the focus of so much attention.

During the twelve-year presidency of Franklin Roosevelt, spanning most of the Great Depression and World War II, the office became the center of the U.S. political universe. Subsequent to that, during the administration of John Kennedy in the early 1960s, the office underwent a near apotheosis, with the news media covering every move of the president and his glamorous wife. Just as the presidency was reaching its greatest glory, it was brought down to its knees in the wake of the abuses of power, corruption, and failures of Lyndon Johnson and Richard Nixon during the Vietnam War and Watergate in the 1960s and early 1970s. At the same time, primaries fast were becoming the predominant means by which states selected their delegates to the national conventions.

These events taken together are important, because presidents and candidates for president were gaining more and more prominence and attention during the never-ending primary-laden campaigns and while in office just as the political system was suffering the consequences of too much power residing in an office occupied by one man. To many observers, it seemed that the trends in presidential nomination politics in the direction of more and more democracy—perhaps an excess of democracy—were at cross-purposes with the need to de-emphasize the office and scale down its powers. Some observers felt that the future of the republic was at stake in the crisis of public authority that came with the failure in Vietnam and the scandals surrounding the Watergate break-in.

This chapter lays out the range of thinking about presidential nomination politics in recent years, summarizing the scholarly debates over the desirability of plebiscitary nomination campaigns. It lays out the arguments for and against the current nomination process. Ultimately it will define what constitutes a constructive environment for public decision making in a presidential nomination campaign. Last, it looks at some of the more commonly proposed and popular proposals to reform presidential nomination campaigns.

Introduction

The changes in the presidential nomination process have, since the early 1970s, been subject to a constant barrage of criticism. The culmination of the changes in the nomination process that occurred in the 1970s left the organizational party out of the mix almost altogether. The relatively unfettered competition among candidate-centered campaign organizations that characterizes the process led to warnings by academics of the dangers of too much democracy. Some academics warned especially of a process that, without the restraining influence of the organizational party, was too susceptible to demagoguery.

Some of the most prominent political scientists in the country have warned of dire consequences resulting from the way presidents are selected in the United States. The possible consequences range from presidential incapacity, to a presidency drawn to stir up international incidents at the drop of a hat, to ever more serious constitutional crises—in part because of the minimal role of the institutional political parties in the presidential selection process.

For example, James Ceaser (1979) contends that the traditional parties served as a brake at the national conventions (and in state and local party units across the country) for popular movements toward candidates damaging to the long-term reputation of the party. Ceaser endorses the wisdom of having an institutionalized elite in a position to veto the nomination of a demagogue or incompetent. While the "natural aristocracy" may have served that function in the early days of the republic, his argument goes, the political parties traditionally have served that function since about the 1830s. It was at this time that the party organizations, especially the Democratic one, matured to the point at which they began to institutionalize national conventions and positions of leadership at the state and local levels.

Ceaser maintains that in the modern political milieu, without some form of peer review of candidates, people running for office invariably will resort to demagogic appeals in the public campaigns that determine the nominees. Without peer review from the political parties, there would be no restraints on candidates. Ceaser and others maintain that it is naive to think that voters can know enough about the candidates to be entrusted with an irreversible decision of the magnitude of choosing a presidential candidate out of a large field of contenders. In short, the risk is that dangerous people are too likely to get elected.

Theodore Lowi (1985) extend Ceaser's criticism of the free-for-all nomination process by making even more explicit the dangers inherent in an entirely popularly based presidential selection process. In an era of potential nuclear annihilation, he writes, it is ludicrous to allow a president's only source of support and political capital to come from the public.

Lowi notes that the president's election and re-election today depend entirely on his own efforts; there is no shared responsibility institutionalized in the electoral process. In a purely plebiscitary selection process the eventual president has not been required to develop ties with other powerful politicians. This fact, together with the fact that the president is the only nationally elected official and the public expects so much from him, may lead to the inexorable temptation for a president to take extreme measures to maintain the public support necessary to govern. Presidents, he asserts, increasingly have been drawn into instigating international incidents to shore up this public support. Lowi's contention is that presidents should and must be answerable to elites in their parties during the selection process to assist them in governing. In fact, governing within the U.S. constitutional framework may only be possible if there is a system of shared responsibility and accountability among elites.

Nelson Polsby (1983) and many others stress the point that a candidate needs to develop working relationships with other elites during the campaign to be able to govern effectively and reliably. The party, he says, is the only organization to provide the crucial link between electoral politics and governing. Governing requires working with other politicians, bureaucrats, and interest blocs in Washington and around the country. The best way to govern effectively is to develop relationships with political elites in Congress and at the state and local levels during the campaign. The party provides the framework to make the connection between the campaign and governing. A purely plebiscitary mandate—that is, winning an election by appealing to the public over the heads of the elites—is ephemeral. The public loses interest after a time and may turn on the president shortly after he takes office. As everyone knows, presidents invariably suffer dips in their level of popularity.

Polsby maintains that Jimmy Carter's election was forged almost exclusively in a plebiscitary manner, his election strategy having focused on gathering support based on his personal appeal. His public support, which may always have been shallow, became irrelevant after a short time in office as the public lost interest and eventually turned on him. Carter's electoral coalition had been pieced together with minimal participation from Democratic elites and major interest blocs sympathetic to and willing to work with the party. He quickly found governing very difficult without a reliable base of support among political elites.

Critics such as Ceaser, Lowi, and Polsby say that only the political party can provide the crucial link between getting elected and governing. They say that it is important to put the party back in control of nominating presidential candidates so that candidates are forced to develop the ties with party leaders that make effective governing possible.

However appealing the idea of a return to party-dominated nomination politics may be to some, its resurrection in any recognizable form would be impossible to accomplish. Barring radical constitutional reform, the days of the sort of party control Ceaser and others hark back to cannot be revisited. Politics, governing, and campaigns *at all levels everywhere in the country* are not controlled or dependent on the institutional parties. Governing is not, and has not been for some time, about rallying party-based majorities. Our politics have been fractured and fragmented for decades; the party had been removed as a controlling influence in nomination politics at other levels of government long before it finally was removed in presidential politics. However regrettable it is, parties cannot be brought back to anything resembling their previous form on any permanent basis.

It is interesting, as any close observer of U.S. politics knows, that the organizational party in many ways has far more resources at its disposal today than it ever had, but the key point is that its *role in our politics has changed dramatically*, in ways that were outlined in chapter 2. It no longer has the direct connections with the people through patronage and government services that it once had. It no longer plays much of a direct role in governing (or, of course, in nomination politics). Instead, it mostly provides ancillary general election campaign services to candidates of the party who must run their primary campaigns without the help of the party. These candidates cannot and do not cede over control of their general election campaigns to the party. In almost every state and community in the nation, the party has no controlling influence.

All of these developments may be unfortunate. In fact, there is a school of thought that believes that it is the weakness of our parties that has led directly to so many of the problems in contemporary U.S. politics, including gridlock, the excessive and pernicious influence of special interests on public policy, the persistently high and debilitating deficits, and the generally fractious nature of our national politics. These are legitimate and perhaps properly diagnosed complaints. The weakness of parties may very well be an important part of these problems—and many more to boot. This school of thought, which could be said to be spearheaded by the distinguished political scientist James Sundquist, has advocated for some years constitutional reform moving in the direction of parliamentary democracy to revivify parties.

There are good arguments to be made for such reform, but such reforms must be considered extraordinarily unlikely to be enacted, partly because they may not be that popular and partly because of the obstacles in the system to any constitutional changes. Because of this, presidential nomination politics in this country is and will continue to be plebiscitary in character. However unfortunate this may be, our nomination politics is a process of *public choice*. It can be analyzed appropriately only on that basis. Just because it has taken on a permanently plebiscitary character does not mean it cannot be improved. After all, there are many possible forms of direct, plebiscitary democracy. The important point is that if ordinary citizens are to have this crucial role of direct participation in the nomination of presidential candidates, they certainly should be afforded the opportunity to consider carefully, and perhaps even reconsider, the alternatives presented to them. Much more is said on this subject later.

But first, a closer look at the debates that rage in the journalistic, scholarly, and political community about the quality of the campaign environment that exists in presidential nomination campaigns—both in terms of the quality of the decision making by the voters and the quality of the institutional arrangements in the process—will help define what constitutes a constructive campaign environment for public participation in presidential nomination campaigns. Later sections will take a look at some of the popular and frequently proposed reform alternatives.

The Debates about the Process

The way our parties go about nominating presidential candidates has been the source of almost endless debate among journalists, scholars, and politicians over the last twenty years or so. Observers have quarreled over the quality of the discourse in these campaigns, the quality of the decision making by the public, and the quality of the people who choose to run.

What follows is a summary of the debates about presidential primaries on these topics. The format is to juxtapose competing arguments that address the same issues. The arguments supportive of the basic form of the current presidential nomination process appear first, followed by the rebutting arguments of critics of the process. The positions are derived from many academic and journalistic sources.

1. Is Participatory Democracy Desirable?

Participation for participation's sake: For citizens to be meaningful participants in a democracy, they must have direct input in choosing their leaders. All the way back to the ancient Greeks, it has been recognized that the maximum participation in civic affairs on the part of the public is desirable and an integral part of the lives of free citizens—in fact, an important aspect of any thinking person's self-actualization. Whenever feasible, in important matters, citizens should have direct impact on the choice of their leaders. In U.S. politics we have seen that it is feasible to have citizen participation in the nomination process. Denying citizens the right to participate directly in intraparty affairs denies them an important component of self-rule.

There can be too much democracy: Participation in civic affairs is obviously desirable, but it is not always possible for citizens to know everything they need to know about a presidential candidate. A politician's peers may be the only ones to know relevant aspects of a politician's life and work. Public participation is important in nomination politics, but there must be some opportunity built into a process for people in the know to veto choices made too hastily by an electorate without access to information only available to those who have worked with the candidates over the course of many years. In essence, there needs to be some check on the decision-making power of the public in a decision as consequential as the selection of presidential candidates.

The prudent citizen recognizes the desirability of limits to self-rule. Just because it is feasible to conduct intraparty democracy does not mean it is desirable to do so. As long as citizens have the power in the general election to choose their leaders, it is not an infringement on self-rule to have a less than purely democratic and participatory nomination process.

2. Is the Process *Too* Open?

Two choices are not enough: The process of nominating and electing a presidential candidate used to leave the public, in most election years, with only two choices—the Democratic and Republican nominee. Since the 1850s, only Democrats and Republicans have had legitimate chances to be elected president. We have had, and will likely always have, a two-party system. The single-member-district, winner-take-all structure of U.S. elections militates strongly in favor of the maintenance of the two-party system, hence the existence of only two real choices on election day.

Most democratic countries present their voters with more than two viable choices in national elections. In a country as large and diverse as ours, ethnically, regionally, and economically, restricting choices offered to the public to two is likely to cause some groups to feel excluded from the process; in fact, it is very likely to have the effect of systematically excluding groups of people from any meaningful participation. Oligarchic control of the elite machinery of the two parties was maintained in the past to the exclusion of certain groups in the population. An obvious example was the lack of any meaningful representation in either party for black Americans from about 1880 until well into the 1930s, when Roosevelt's New Deal brought a few blacks into the Democratic fold. In fact, the Democratic party organizations in the southern states existed in large measure for the *express purpose* of excluding blacks from the political process.

The system of primaries and open caucuses opens up the parties to *anyone* who is able to organize and get his or her name on the ballot. In recent years diverse groups that likely would have remained on the fringes of our politics have found access and influence through the candidacies of Jesse Jackson on the Democratic side and Pat Robertson on the Republican side. A system that otherwise would limit choice to two is made healthier by giving voters in the presidential primaries far more choices and avenues for participation.

Parties have no responsibility to open themselves up to any movement: For political parties to operate meaningfully in a democratic polity, they must adhere to some sort of principle, principles, or program. Unfortunately, the trend in contemporary U.S. politics has been to make "openness" the only principle of the parties; this is especially true of the Democrats. Parties that are as open as ours are in no position to carry through a principled agenda when elected to control the government. The parties become vehicles of cults of personality, not organizations committed to a set of principles that could serve the country well on a lasting basis. For parties to maintain any integrity or value they must be able to *exclude* those who do not adhere to their lasting principles.

The U.S. political system *was* too closed before the opening of the parties, but not because the parties were exclusive. The fact that Americans were limited to two choices was not a good thing, and it was perpetuated by unconstitutional laws that forbade third parties on the ballots in many states. (Such laws were commonly put into place around the turn of the century in the very states in which third-party movements presented a threat to the established parties.) The useful remedy to the limitation on choice in elections was achieved in the courtrooms of the country by third-party presidential candidates George Wallace in 1968 and John Anderson in 1980. Those two guaranteed with their litigation reasonable access to the ballots of all fifty states for third-party movements. The best evidence of the ease of access is the ability of little-known and modestly funded Lenora Fulani to get on the ballot in all the fifty states in recent presidential elections.

The solution to the problem of limited choice has been achieved by allowing third-party movements access to the ballot and the opportunity to form and compete in national elections, as they have done. The correct solution is not what actually has happened—gutting the existing major parties and removing any coherent set of principles by opening them up to anyone who wishes to call himself or herself a Democrat or Republican.

3. Should Anyone Be Able to Become President?

Give little-knowns a chance: One of the beauties of the open nomination process as it currently is arranged is that it gives a wide range of people the opportunity to become president. The small early states give a heretofore little-known person the fair opportunity to make his or her case for the nomination. The public is not limited to insiders and long-time politicians in its choices for the highest office in the land. Great leaders are not necessarily famous. This process gives the public a chance to consider senators, governors, or other people who are not household names. These fresh new faces may, at times, provide the kind of leadership the people are looking for *and that the country needs.* Picking only from among prominent party leaders, as was commonly done in the past, is not always desirable. It is precisely this sort of process that has produced some of our *least* successful presidents, such as Lyndon Johnson and Richard Nixon.

The opportunity to become president is not an entitlement: There is no reason that a country with the power to eliminate mankind with nuclear weapons must give someone the opportunity to become president who has not been in the public eye, serving the nation, for many years. No other democracy lets *anyone* be in the position to be chief executive. Our current system is profoundly unwise in that it does not require long-time service before serious consideration can be given for an established party's nomination. It is critical, when the stakes are so high, that some opportunity for peer review gets institutionalized. A process that lets anyone become president is an inherently dangerous one.

Furthermore, Bartels and others have demonstrated that some voters make their choices in the primaries without much information about some of the candidates. Voters frequently vote for someone they know little about, if only because they are an alternative to some other candidate. This leaves open the real possibility that voters could select a nominee without giving the proper consideration to his or her qualifications to lead the free world. An obviously uninformed electorate cannot choose wisely among the numerous candidates running in most nomination races.

4. Are Iowa and New Hampshire Good Early Tests?

The small states are good early testing grounds for presidential candidates: Iowa and New Hampshire, while they do not make many presidential candidacies, do break a lot of them. They serve the useful purpose of weeding out the trial-balloon candidacies that do not wear well under the intense scrutiny they receive in these states. As such, these two states have a great deal of impact on who will be the next president.

To have small states weed out the field of candidates eliminates many of the negative aspects of mass political campaigning. In these small states, the voters get an extended opportunity to evaluate, and even to meet, the candidates. The premium is on retail politicking, not the thirty-second commercial, and on organizational skills, not massive advertising purchases. The voters in these states pride themselves on their attentiveness to the nomination process, and they make informed choices. It is better that the nomination not automatically go to the richest candidate, as it would were large states to lead off the campaign—states that could be "bought" with expensive media buys. In Iowa and New Hampshire almost any candidate can afford to campaign and get known and get a campaign off the ground. The emphasis on Iowa and New Hampshire makes for a fairer process and a process where informed decision making and retail politicking—not sound-bite politicking—play a significant role.

There is far too much emphasis on small, unrepresentative states: States such as Iowa and New Hampshire have populations that are strikingly homogeneous from an ethnic and racial standpoint. Furthermore, these states are less blue collar and far more rural than the rest of the country. They are about as unrepresentative of the country as any. There is little economic diversity or diversity of interests. The emphasis on Iowa and New Hampshire places some candidates at a distinct advantage over others, because of regional or ideological proximity to the voters who live in these states.

In Iowa in particular, with the precinct caucus forum for participation, only the most attentive, and disproportionately the most ideological, voters participate, further skewing an already unrepresentative state. These states take on tremendous importance because they are a necessary publicity springboard for success in later larger states and multiple primary days that follow shortly after them. The bias inherent in having states such as these play such a prominent role can be and should be corrected.

5. Is the Mass Media Emphasis in the Process Desirable?

The ability to communicate on television is an important part of the campaign and of governing: While critics rue the inevitable saturation of the mass media by presidential candidates in these campaigns, the reality is that presidents while in office must be or learn to be compelling communicators to push through an agenda successfully. The public expects the president to lead the country in a variety of domestic areas, and of course he must lead in the case of a foreign crisis. No matter whether one thinks this is a regrettable development, the reality is that a critical part of providing the leadership is rallying the public on television. Surely one of the reasons that Reagan achieved so much of his agenda (and Bush achieved so little) was because of his communication skills.

The mass media emphasis in the primaries tests a vital quality of successful governance. Of course, Bush's success in the primaries indicates that communication skills are not necessarily decisive in these races. But this does not diminish the fact that communication skills are tested, and such skills also are of critical importance to a president while in office.

Too much of an emphasis on the mass media leads to a reliance on gimmicks and may lead to dangerous demagoguery: The public often is presented with several candidates from which to choose in the primaries, sometimes as many as a half-dozen or more in the same party. Many of the candidates are rather obscure figures before the presidential race (some obscure people have gone on to win in the primaries; some even have become president), and sometimes the views of the candidates on the major issues of the day are very similar.

As a result, there often is little to distinguish the contenders except some gimmick or fad or catchy slogan. Unfortunately, the best scenario involves harmless gimmicks ("The Massachusetts Miracle"—Dukakis '88; a bow tie— Simon '88; an 800 number—Brown '92) or catchy but meaningless slogans ("New Ideas"—Hart '88; "A Candidate We Don't Have to Train"—Bush '80). The real danger lies in demagogic approaches to distinguishing one's candidacy. Mass media campaigning is inevitable in the contemporary age, but every effort should be made to structure the process to lessen the need for it in the nomination campaign. Otherwise, as is developing, candidates are forced to resort to sloganeering and demagoguery. Communication skills *are* an important part of the presidency. Consideration of them should wait until the general election campaign.

6. Do Voters Learn about the Next President?

The long grueling campaign allows the voters to learn valuable information about the candidates for president: It reasonably could be argued that the campaign trail is too long, but there are considerable advantages to an extended nomination campaign period. Voters do get the opportunity to learn about the candidates' positions, career accomplishments, and character. The presidency itself is a grueling job, fraught with difficulties of an international, domestic, and political scope. If one cannot withstand the pressures of the campaign, it surely is logical that one could not withstand the pressures of leading the country and the free world. If a candidate has some character flaws that would disqualify him from office that have remained hidden because of a lack of scrutiny in the past, the nomination campaign surely will expose them. We can never guarantee that we will avoid presidents with unstable or dangerous temperaments, but surely the sort of campaign we now have will reduce greatly the probability that we elect one.

It is an empirical question as to whether voters actually do learn about the candidates' positions and backgrounds, but the opportunity is there. If voters are not availing themselves of the opportunity, they should. Citizens in a democracy have a responsibility soberly to consider the qualifications of the people running. One would be hard-pressed to devise a process that provides more opportunities to meet, see, hear debate among, and consider informed opinion about the candidates.

The nomination process is so long it discourages good candidates, and voters do not have the opportunity to learn relevant information about the candidates: It is a myth that voters have a reasonable opportunity soberly to consider the qualifications of the candidates. As Bartels and others point out, sometimes it takes a while for people to evaluate carefully a list of candidates. Some races for the nomination are decided very quickly, with most of the candidates in a party (sometimes all but one—the nominee) eliminated within a few weeks. Voters in some states may have to make a decision very early, before important relevant information comes to light, and those in other states that have primaries later may be presented with a sharply reduced list of candidates to choose from or may even be presented with no choice at all.

It also is important to emphasize that much of the media coverage focuses on the results of the latest primaries and on polling results. Neither of these pieces of information provides relevant data to the public about the careers, character, or accomplishments of the candidates. Voters would have to be very selective about their consumption of news to get good substantial information on career accomplishments, positions on issues, and character.

And while character issues obviously are of tremendous importance in considering presidential candidates, much of the media's fascination with character revolves around titillating scandals, and not the tougher but more relevant character questions involving, for example, a candidate's perseverance in pursuing and following through on an agenda in Congress or in a statehouse. The quality of the presidential nomination process depends too much on a media driven by making a fast buck.

It also should be noted that the nomination process is grueling in a much different way from the presidency. The nomination campaign is an endurance test, lasting far longer than the three and a half months of primaries. For a year or more prior to Iowa and New Hampshire candidates must crisscross the country in a search for money and support. Such a process probably discourages many of our most qualified politicians, who may specialize in crafting policy proposals, dealing with other politicians, and formulating new approaches to foreign policy. Our better potential leaders may not relish the thought of having to raise money constantly for an uncertain and often degrading delegate selection process.

7. Is the Campaign a Learning Process for the Candidates?

Presidents need to be in touch with the people's problems and concerns: Although presidential campaigns had few primaries in 1960, John Kennedy, who was about as far removed from poverty as a person could be, benefited from the opportunity to meet coal miners and see the conditions they lived and worked in when he was a candidate for the Democratic nomination. Fortunately there was a hotly contested primary in West Virginia that year, and Kennedy was given the opportunity to learn about a group of fellow Americans he might never otherwise have come in contact with. The campaign was no burden for Jimmy Carter either, sixteen years later. He regarded it as an opportunity to meet and get in touch with people in parts of the country about which he had relatively little knowledge.

The president represents all of the people. Today's campaign requires the candidates to get out among the people all around the country. We always should keep in mind that politics is emphatically not strictly a matter of high-minded debates about public policy. Politics is about values and interests, as well as issues, and issue positions are not merely analytical questions. Politicians need to feel and experience the problems they will have to address. There is no substitute for going around the country and meeting with concerned citizens for the year or two prior to the election. This kind of campaign, while grueling, is exactly the sort of thing that best prepares presidents to work on the people's business.

The campaign is too hectic and too grueling: There is, of course, considerable benefit to meeting and listening to people at the grass roots level, but most of the campaigning in most of the states is done from tarmacs and television studios. It simply is impossible, in a country the size of ours, for a candidate to get any meaningful sense of the problems of all of the people. The nomination campaign is, in fact, reduced to superficial televised forums and speeches at airports, and a great deal of the candidates' time is spent raising money; it is not spent in worthwhile give-and-take with the nation's citizens.

Some contact with people is better for a future president than none but the price we have paid for the interminably long and grueling campaigns is great. Some people evidently thrive on nonstop campaigning for president for an entire year, but the process of airport hopping and endless fund-raisers probably has discouraged some of our best and brightest from pursuing the White House. It is obvious that the endless scrutiny and campaigning require a type of stamina that may not be relevant at all to the serious work of governing, such as working with Congress, working with the bureaucracy, and making good appointments to positions in government. Many of the politicians who might best be able to fulfill the duties of the presidency probably are ruled out of consideration.

What Does a Good Campaign Environment Look Like?

These seven debates bring up a great many intriguing issues in nomination politics. It is particularly important to focus on what these debates say about what constitutes a good campaign environment.

Debates (1) and (2) revolve around the desirability of public participation at this phase of the selection of a president. The fact is that presidential nomination campaigns are plebiscitary, and as long as the Democratic and Republican parties dominate U.S. politics they will remain that way; after all, the parties were able to retain their dominance in the political system *because* of their willingness to open up their proceedings. The real challenge, therefore, is to improve the opportunity for the public to make good choices. If there are shortcomings in the process, a second challenge is to identify precisely those shortcomings and to investigate whether it is possible to correct them.

What the American public should aim for in presidential nomination campaigns is a context that allows for fair and responsible public choice. The following are key characteristics of such a context:

1. The electoral arrangements in the process must be fair to the candidates, and votes must be tallied fairly and democratically.
2. Given the commonly large fields of candidates, the public must have a reasonable opportunity to learn about the issue positions, accomplishments, and character of the people running. Candidates, as well, must have a reasonable opportunity to learn the concerns of the public.
3. The process should not permit hastily made judgments to dictate the nomination of a presidential candidate. Because of the high stakes in presidential selection, the public must be given the opportunity to reconsider its initial judgments of the candidates.
4. The process must not have obstacles to entry for candidates that are so burdensome that they discourage the candidacy of potentially good candidates.

Reform Options

The presidential nomination process as a method of public choice has come under heavy fire. One of its many curious characteristics is that it really has not been planned or organized intentionally into its current form. It has become what it is on an ad hoc basis, the result of a series of incremental reforms in response to political upheaval and changes in communications and campaign technology.

What has evolved is fundamentally an electoral system—a method of public choice. Hence, it should be scrutinized as such, and not as it traditionally has been described—as a representative process of selecting delegates for the purpose of a deliberative convention. No deliberation happens anymore; the real decision is made in an unorganized, haphazard series of plebiscitary events. This process may have some good qualities, but if this is the case, it is mostly by accident!

Many reformers contend that it would be wise to reconsider and restructure the way that candidates are nominated by the parties. Many even go so far as to say that since the presidential nomination process has become, for all intents and purposes, a public question, and not primarily an intraparty affair, it should become the business of the U.S. Congress to reform it.

In any event, obviously the stakes are large in this debate. The next section looks at three popular reform alternatives. All have been advanced by journalists, politicians, or academics, or some combination of those three sources. They carry the common theme that a method of public choice of this importance should be instituted with proper consideration of ends and means, instead of by incremental, illthought out ad hoc procedures. Three of the most popular comprehensive reform alternatives are described below, along with the case for their adoption. In chapters 7 and 8 they are subjected to critical analysis.

The National Primary

The institution of a national primary would alter radically the nature of presidential nomination politics. Such an event would eliminate completely any pretense of representative democracy in nomination politics. Essentially, nominations by the major parties for president would be conducted as nominations for other federal offices are in almost all of the states—by means of a single plebiscite.

A national primary would merge all the fifty state delegate selection events into a one-day event in the first week of June, to determine popularly the presidential nominees of the parties. Conventions would be held in July and August as they are now, but their purpose would be solely to conduct other party business, such as platform planks and the selection of the vice presidential candidate.

There are a couple of different ways that a national primary could be enacted. Court rulings in recent years have supported the national parties' right to dictate rules of delegate selection to the states. Either of the national parties then could, in theory, stipulate that a single-day primary (perhaps better thought of as fifty state primaries on one day) be held, with delegates selected in each state bound by the outcome of the event proportional to the votes cast in the state. It probably is reasonable to assume that if either party enacted a national primary, the other would find it very difficult to resist joining it. The way delegates currently are selected would appear corrupt and anachronistic in comparison to the national primary.

Some advocates of a national primary propose that the best way for such a reform to be implemented would be by means of an act of Congress, making the event a truly national election. This would remove the complications of delegate selection and rules governing how delegates are allotted. Presumably Congress only would enact such a law with the assurance that the parties would abide by the outcome of the primary in their selection of the nominees.

Such a national election would be like a presidential election, with some variations. To make the primary more accessible to lesser-known candidates, federally financed television time would need to be provided by Congress for candidates qualifying for matching funds under the current rules (see chapters 2 and 3). This would come in the form of discounted advertising rates during the national primary campaign. There also could be a series of nationally sponsored debates for the candidates receiving matching funds.

Most advocates of a national primary support the possibility of having a run-off primary. This would take place between the top two finishers three weeks after the first primary in the event that no candidate polled at least 40 percent of the vote in the first primary. For purposes of this discussion, the national primary will be considered as a one-day, congressionally mandated event, with the possibility of a run-off primary if no candidate receives 40 percent of the vote.

Advocates of the national primary reform cite four main advantages. First, the length of the public phase of the campaign surely would be reduced. It would lessen significantly the furious and seemingly endless grind of the single-state primaries that occur week after week from February until June in the current arrangements. Second, they cite its fairness relative to the current setup, which puts small numbers of voters, particularly in Iowa and New Hampshire, in an advantaged position and renders irrelevant the participation of many voters in states that hold primaries after most of the candidates have been eliminated. Third, such a reform lends some rationality to a process that is little understood by the general population. Most voters in the current process of serialized primaries and precinct caucuses have little idea what their participation means; they might not even focus on the fact that they are contributing to the selection of the next president. The national primary event would have a clear and evident purpose. Last, and following from the third point, there is a good chance that a national primary would focus voters' attention nationally. Candidates would be given scrutiny by the voters across the country that they only get in a few areas of the country with the current process. More voters might then have the opportunity to learn of the candidates' issue positions, accomplishments, and character.

Convention/National Primary

Thomas Cronin (most prominently—there are other advocates) has come up with perhaps the most radical of reform alternatives to the presidential nomination process. In an effort to preserve, and actually to enhance, the role of the organizational party in nomination politics, Cronin suggests having the national conventions *prior* to a national primary. The purpose of the conventions would be to select two or three candidates to compete in the national primary.

This reform idea has taken many different forms. In all its formulations, the national conventions would change in character considerably. Some would have the state parties select delegates to the national convention in the traditional process of caucuses and conventions leading up to a state convention, at which the delegation finally would be selected. The national convention then would vote to select two or three candidates for a national primary.

In another, more radical formulation (and the one considered here), the national conventions would be gatherings of the fifty state party central committees. The state committee members would have their votes at the national convention weighted according to national party rules, based primarily on population. The national conventions, held in July of the presidential election year, would be an occasion for the convention participants from the fifty state central committees to cast their votes for presidential candidates. Any candidates receiving more than 25 percent of the vote at the convention would compete in a national primary to be held in the first week of September.

If only one candidate reached the 25 percent threshold, and he or she received a majority (the term *majority* is properly defined as *50 percent plus one;* the term *plurality* refers to a winning first-place margin *that need not reach 50 percent*) of the vote, he or she would be the nominee without a primary. Also, any candidate receiving two-thirds of the convention vote could avoid a primary. If only one candidate received greater than 25 percent, but less than 50 percent, then subsequent balloting would be held to produce competitors for the front-runner or to secure the nomination if he or she can reach the two-thirds special majority or the 50 percent threshold without another candidate getting the necessary 25 percent.

This would result in either two or three candidates competing in a national primary in September. The candidates' campaigns would be federally financed, but the parties would be responsible for providing forums or debates, as they deemed necessary. The top vote getter in the primary, regardless of percentage, would be the party's nominee. There would be no run-off stipulation.

Advocates of this reform of presidential nomination politics cite several advantages. Typically they are deeply concerned about the systemic consequences the removal of the organizational party from nomination politics has had on the ability of presidents to govern, as well as on the political system more broadly. They see this reform as staking out a valuable middle ground that maintains a strictly plebiscitary element with the possibility of a national primary while bringing back a strong role for the organizational party. The party regulars would exercise their power by ratifying the choices the public would have for the national primary.

Also, convention/national primary reformers point to the benefits of reinstitution of peer review. The idea is that voters do not have the opportunity to know much about the character of the candidates. Presumably insiders would be in a better position to use their judgment to weed out candidates who might not be fit to serve as president for some reason.

Another advantage frequently mentioned is the reduction in the number of candidates that voters have to consider in the popular part of the nomination process. Limiting the field to two or three candidates can allow candidates to draw meaningful distinctions between or among themselves. This way they would not have to rely on gimmicks, as is common in large fields of candidates in the current campaigns, or as likely would happen in a national primary such as that proposed earlier. Another advantage is that the convention/national primary would shorten the public phase of the campaign season considerably.

There would be less emphasis on money raising with the public financing of the national primary, and the national primary and general election campaigns both would be shortened considerably.

Regional Primaries

A popular reform that alters the current process less radically than the two alternatives previously described is that of regional primaries. To lend rationality to the ordering of events and to stem the tendency toward front-loading now occurring in the process, a series of five ten-state regional primaries would be instituted.

In its most common incarnation, the five primaries would be arranged three weeks apart, starting on the first Tuesday of March and finishing at the end of May. The country would be divided into five regions, as indicated in table 4.1. The order of the regional events would rotate in each presidential election year.

This reform could be implemented by one of the parties, acting within its powers by dictating when states can hold primary elections. More efficiently perhaps, an act of Congress could dictate the ordering of events, bringing the parties into line by requiring adherence to the plan for the party's candidate to receive federal funding in the general election. Parties would be left free to decide for themselves exactly how to allocate delegates on the basis of the primary outcomes; as it is done now, state parties use their discretion, subject to national party rules. Campaign finance rules would remain as they are now. Conventions would retain their current role, which in recent years has amounted to ratifying the decision made by voters in primaries.

As one can see, this reform is nowhere near as radical as the two previous ones. Instead of instituting a national plebiscite (as both of the previous ones do), or attempting to revivify the party organizations (as the convention/national primary reform does), this reform simply attempts to lend some rationality to the ordering of the primary events, which today are arranged almost entirely on an ad hoc basis. The major alteration would be to require primaries in the states.

Second in importance to that is the dictating of the dates of the primaries. As mentioned above, the parties in the states would retain discretion over delegate allocation and selection methods. The advantage of instituting only relatively minor changes is that there will be fewer unforeseen consequences than with the other more radical reforms. Surely whatever advantages the current system offers would be lost with a national primary, but they might be retained with less-radical reform as represented here with regional primaries.

As mentioned above, advocates of reform cite the advantages of imposing some order and rationality on the free-for-all process of scheduling primaries and precinct caucuses. Currently the Democratic national party does impose a loose window of three months (first week of March through the first week of June) during which states can select delegates, but it has allowed several exemptions, most notably to Iowa and New Hampshire, to allow them to retain their traditional starting positions. The regional primaries concept would eliminate the advantage that these two small states have, which many allege skews the process in favor of candidates from these regions and leaves voters in other states with less of an impact on the outcome of the race.

Table 4.1
Regional primaries

REGION I **West**

Hawaii, Alaska, Washington, Oregon, California, Idaho, Nevada, Utah, Arizona, Montana, Wyoming, Colorado, New Mexico

REGION II **Central States**

North Dakota, South Dakota, Nebraska, Kansas, Oklahoma, Texas, Minnesota, Iowa, Missouri

REGION III **South**

Arkansas, Louisiana, Tennessee, Mississippi, Alabama, Georgia, Florida, South Carolina, North Carolina, Virginia

REGION IV **Midwest/Mid-Atlantic**

Wisconsin, Illinois, Michigan, Indiana, Kentucky, Ohio, West Virginia, Maryland

REGION V **Northeast**

Pennsylvania, Delaware, New York, New Jersey, Connecticut, Rhode Island, Massachusetts, Vermont, New Hampshire, Maine

---

Perhaps the most important advantage of the regional primaries reform, according to its advocates, relates to its mandated spacing of the five primaries three weeks apart. The process of front-loading would be ended. In the current process, there has evolved a scramble among states to move their primaries up in the calendar to benefit from the attention that early states get. This has culminated with the movement of the California primary from June to March (see chapter 2).

There are two problems with front-loading. One is that few candidates can afford to campaign in so many states that early in the campaign. Early fund-raising, before any primaries have taken place, becomes even more of an advantage than it already is. Second is that the crush of early primaries seems to determine the nominee very early in the process, as could be seen in the 1988 Republican contest (with Bush eliminating most of the competition in March) and the 1992 Democratic contest (in which most of Clinton's competition fell by the wayside by early April). This happens because most of the candidates (perhaps all but one) are forced to drop out of the campaign. This has the potential to give the voters in later states no say and, most important, little opportunity to review and reconsider the qualifications of the candidates. (Remember that many successful candidates are all but unknown prior to their early successes. Voters have difficulty digesting information about these candidates in any meaningful way in a short period of time.) The opportunity for sober reflection had been one of the main advantages of the current *ad hoc* arrangements; regional primaries advocates maintain that this advantage is seriously jeopardized by the trend toward front-loading. This opportunity for more serious and sustained consideration of the candidates by the voters might be maintained, they say, with sufficient spacing between regional primary events.

Conclusion

The plebiscitary presidential nomination process has generated considerable debate and criticism in recent decades. Many observers, attribute to it many of the ills in the political system. While these criticisms may be overblown, certainly an institution with the importance of this one deserves a high level of scrutiny.

The section entitled "debates," addresses several issues concerning presidential nomination campaigns. At the most basic level, two fundamental theoretical questions were raised: Is intraparty democracy a good thing? and Is the current method of intraparty democracy a good one? Whatever one thinks of intraparty democracy in principle, it is a permanent part of our political system as long as these two parties survive. As such, it is more appropriate to focus on the second question—and proceed to evaluate the quality of the current method of public choice and compare it to potential alternatives

The current process has been criticized vigorously (prompting calls for comprehensive reform), primarily for the emphasis placed on Iowa and New Hampshire and the process of front-loading, which, as it reels out of control, may have handicapped the public's ability soberly to undertake its decision-making responsibility. These issues will be revisited in chapters 7 and 8, which compare the current process to the reform options introduced here.

But first, chapter 5 considers another perspective on the campaign environment that was raised in this chapter: that the electoral arrangements in the campaign be fair—especially the way in which the votes of the public are counted.

Chapter Five

An Introduction to Public Choice and Presidential Primaries

In the last forty years or so the *public choice* school of thought was developed and has grown within the disciplines of political science and economics. The extent to which this school of thought is applicable to a wide range of social questions is by no means a settled question, but in political science this approach and similar ones based on economic theories have been very prominent and proven very useful. Although the public choice approach has not become the dominant paradigm in the discipline, it has nearly as many well-regarded adherents at the best universities in the country as any other.

One of the components of public choice particularly applicable to political questions is *social choice theory*. Social choice theorists look at and evaluate the processes by which the public goes about making its decisions when confronted with choices, either in the political or economic realm. In electoral politics, social choice theory looks in a detailed, technical, and formal way at how fairly voters' preferences are aggregated and counted.

In the 1940s and 1950s some important discoveries and rediscoveries were made by economists and political scientists in this area. These discoveries enabled scholars to look far more analytically at the way elections are conducted. Of particular note are some of the findings of Kenneth Arrow, who pioneered this area of study. He demonstrates exactly why elections are not the technically fair instruments for the public to use in making choices that many assumed they were. He shows, among other things, how electoral procedures could be unreliable or can be manipulated by sophisticated people—to the extent that in most real-world cases it actually is impossible to put much faith in their fairness. From this discovery sprouted a raft of studies that effectively put under a microscope the way voters' preferences are translated into outcomes, that is, winners and losers, in elections. This is the essence of social choice theory as it applies to elections—the study of how fairly or democratically the voters' preferences are translated into outcomes. It goes almost without saying that processes of public choice should be conducted fairly.

The next three chapters highlight how the discoveries of the scholars of public choice can be applied to presidential primaries and how these discoveries can inform the debate over the quality of the presidential nomination process. This chapter introduces some of the basic concepts of social choice theory and borrowing from one of the most prominent scholars in the field, develops a set of criteria that can be used to evaluate how fair the process of aggregating the preferences of voters is in presidential primaries.

Introduction

It generally is taken for granted in a democracy that the outcome of an election is a fair reflection of the preferences expressed by voters at the polls. In simple language, most people would say that the winner of an election should be the candidate preferred by more voters than any other candidate. This statement is so obvious that it literally goes without saying in a democracy. This idea is one of the components of a good campaign environment in presidential nomination politics: the electoral arrangements in the process must be fair to the candidates, and votes must be tallied fairly and democratically.

In analyzing elections and campaigns, interested observers ordinarily complain about and criticize all aspects of elections *except* whether the tallying of the votes reflects the preferences of the voters as they view the the candidates on the ballot on election day. People debate endlessly the impact of money or special interests on an election, the use of dirty tactics, whether some candidates have fair access to the ballot, whether some potential voters can register easily, and countless other things. Certainly those are all profoundly important questions in any democracy. But whether the winner is the candidate most preferred by the voters among those on the ballot is rarely questioned. In other words, the fairness of the way votes are counted is not commonly a matter of debate.

But this question is one of the foremost concerns of scholars of public choice. They have maintained for many years that the one thing most people counted on about elections—that the voters, however swayed or manipulated during the sound and fury of the campaign, did end up preferring the winning candidate to the others—is open to question in many elections.

Looking at this in another way, public choice theorists point out that even in a perfect world in which all candidates had equal access to the media, the candidates all conducted fair and issue-oriented campaigns, and all voters were attentive, thoughtful, and informed and they all were satisfied with the choices offered, the outcome of the election may not be an accurate reflection of the voters' preferences and attitudes about the candidates. To borrow from E.E. Schattschneider, even if the country had 250,000,000 Aristotles, it cannot necessarily be said that the winners and losers actually should have won and lost!

For the purpose of argument, consider the idea of the perfect campaign environment. The fact is that, as public choice theorists have demonstrated, in this hypothetical environment the *only* time it can be said with confidence that the outcome of the election reflects the preferences of the voters is when there are only two candidates running. In this situation, the public can be confident that the majority winner is preferred by the voters on election day to the other candidate. But *any* time there are more than two candidates competing there is a significant chance that the candidate most preferred by the voters will not win.

In the United States, the selection process narrows the field of major candidates in most elections in most states for most offices down to two, usually one Democratic and one Republican. Tradition and the structure of the electoral process militate in favor of two-major-party elections. The system does not guarantee two parties, but it does encourage the existence of only two parties and discourage the proliferation of new major parties. U.S. general elections tend to be between two major candidates, and the outcome (barring fraud) reflects the preferences of the voters on election day. (Again, this ignores the debates about how those preferences were formed—whether through manipulative advertising or otherwise—and focuses solely on the fairness of the outcome of the preferences tallied on election day.) To repeat, only elections with just two candidates can be relied on to be fair in the strict sense that is meant here.

How do the choices get narrowed down to two in U.S. politics? Usually, in most states in races for most offices, the process of winnowing the field of candidates to two occurs in primary elections. These elections frequently have more than two candidates competing. The first-place finisher, that is, the candidate who receives the most votes on primary day regardless of the percentage of the vote he or she gets, is awarded the nomination. (Some states, mostly in the south, still retain rules that allow for runoffs if no candidate receives a threshold of 50 percent or 40 percent of the vote. This rule does not apply in presidential primaries in these states.)

The fact is that multicandidate elections, defined as those elections having more than two candidates competing, actually are quite common in U.S. politics. They happen every election year in most states in many primaries. General election campaigns also sometimes involve more than just the two candidates from the major parties. (More than one-third of the presidential elections in U.S. history were contested by more than two major candidates; many times the winner garnered below 50 percent of the vote.) And, of course, many presidential nomination races feature more than two prominent candidates. The unfortunate, inescapable fact is that the outcome of any multicandidate race does not reflect the preferences of the voters with the same certainty that the outcome of a two-candidate race does. The next section examine why that is.

Counting Votes in Multicandidate Elections

In a two-candidate race, a voter, employing his or her rational faculties, casts his or her vote for the candidate that he or she prefers. The calculation is rather simple and obvious for most voters in our general election campaigns, which usually have only two major candidates.

In a race with three candidates the voter's calculation may become far more complicated. Voters may have perfectly rational reasons in a multicandidate race for voting for *someone other than their first choice.* For example, a voter may think her first choice among three candidates has little chance of winning, and she may choose quite rationally to vote for her second choice, to avoid the election of a particularly odious third choice. That sort of voting, referred to as *strategic voting* by social choice theorists, makes it impossible to know whether voters actually are choosing their first choice. Also, voters probably frequently vote for someone who is not really a first choice to send a message to a front-runner or likely winner they may support. Some pundits plausibly suggested that many votes cast for Patrick Buchanan in the 1992 Republican primaries were meant to send a message to President Bush about his breaking his "no new taxes" pledge.

Of course, voters have every right to vote strategically, and it probably goes on quite often. But unlike in the two-candidate race, it is impossible to know in the multicandidate race whether the first-place finisher (the winner in the United States) actually was the first choice of more voters than any other candidate. This fact probably does not bother most people, because it is obvious that the strategic voter described above was acting in her informed best interest to do what she could on election day to defeat her last-choice candidate. Her logic might have been even more compelling if she was convinced that the nomination by her party of the odious third-choice candidate would have led to sure defeat in the general election. There is nothing wrong with voting strategically, even if it makes it impossible to know for sure who had the most "first place" votes. Consider the situation described above diagramatically with a voting population of twelve voters.

V represents the voters [V(1 - 5) represents voters one through five]
A, B, C represent the candidates
1, 2, 3 represent the order of preference by the voters

	1	2	3
V(1 - 5)	A	C	B
V (6 - 9)	B	A	C
V(10 - 12)	C	B	A

The tallying of the first preferences of the voters results in A winning with five voters, to four and three respectively for the other two candidates. Now consider what happens if the strategic voter is one of the voters preferring candidate C. She has seen the pre-election day polls, thinks C's prospects are poor, and wants to make sure that A is not elected. If she and one other C supporter vote for their second choice, B, they can elect B instead of A. In this scenario, B would get six votes, A would get five votes, and C would get one vote

There is nothing wrong with voters doing what the two strategic voters described above did. Basically, because of their sophistication, these two voters allowed this population of voters to choose a candidate, B, that the majority of the voters preferred to the candidate, A, that won when only first choices were tallied. The fact is that candidate B was preferred by more voters than candidate A, but candidate A would have been elected had our two sophisticated voters not voted strategically.

This example demonstrates two of the profound differences between elections with more than two candidates and elections with only two candidates. One is that in multicandidate elections the winner may not be the most preferred candidate. This cannot happen in a two-candidate race. The other is that the outcome of multicandidate elections is potentially manipulable by sophisticated voters. There also is a third profound difference when considering multicandidate elections. Consider again the original set of voter preferences:

	1	2	3
V(1 - 5)	A	C	B
V(6 - 9)	B	A	C
V(10 - 12)	C	B	A

If the set of preferences of the voters in the above scenario is viewed in a different way, and without any strategic voting, a curious situation results. If the candidates are pitted one-on-one in all possible combinations, in a sense, it will be doing in each case what our strategic voters did in the earlier scenario when they took their favorite, C, out of the picture because they perceived that that candidate had no chance of winning.

1. Imagine that candidate A did not exist. A's supporters would support C in the election, since C is their second choice. C then would beat B in a two-candidate race, eight to four.
2. If candidate B does not exist, B's supporters would turn to their second choice, A. A then would defeat candidate C, nine to three.
3. If C did not exist, C's supporters would turn to B (as two of them did in the strategic voting example), and B would defeat A, seven to five.

Here is what results from looking at the preferences of this twelve-person public in this way. C would beat B if those two were paired against each other, B would defeat A in a matchup, and A would defeat C. Scholars of social choice theory sometimes depict these outcomes in this way:

C > B; B > A; A > C or C > B > A > C (that is, *C beats B, who beats A, who in turn can beat C*)

Note in this example that every individual made his or her preferences in a rational or *transitive* ordering. This means that if an individual preferred C to B, and B to A, it was assumed that the individual would prefer C to A. But notice that the whole population—the public—did *not* have a transitive preference ordering. The voters as a whole preferred C to B, and preferred B to A, *but they preferred A to C*—an *intransitive* ordering.

The possibility seems to exist that a population of entirely rational people with transitive preference orderings can produce an intransitive result, in a kind of political version of famous theologian Rheinhold Niebuhr's thesis in his book *Moral Man, Immoral Society.* Public choice scholar Brian Barry, with a play on the title of the Niebuhr work, titled a book on the subject *Rational Man, Irrational Society.* Political scientists usually refer to the situation when a rational citizenry produces an irrational, or intransitive result, as the Paradox of Voting.

Other Methods of Counting Votes

The problems with using the traditional U.S. *single-vote* method of counting votes in multicandidate elections have long been apparent to some people in charge of conducting elections. (The single-vote method used in the United States identifies the winner as the one receiving the most votes from a population permitted to cast just one vote.) In a nutshell, people running elections in politics, in an academic setting, or in other organizations are understandably nervous about proclaiming as the winning alternative or candidate something or someone that receives only a small plurality of the vote.

One of the criticisms of this method is that second, third, and fourth preferences of the voters are not taken into account. The person with the most votes may have far less than a majority of the votes cast and may not have widespread support from across the population. Organizations (or countries, in some cases, for that matter) electing people to leadership positions would like for their leaders to have widespread support. The fear is that the person with the most votes may have the support of only a minority of the population or organizational membership. If a way could be found to consider second and third preferences in the voting, the theory goes, a candidate with broader support could be selected.

An example of an organization that conducts elections for leadership positions in a way that takes into consideration more than the first choice of the relevant electorate is the U.S. House of Representatives. For example, when the Democratic Caucus (the gathering of the Democratic membership) in the House meets to select its leaders, it uses a variant of something called the *Hare* method of voting.

In many cases, if there is an opening for a leadership position, there is a list of several candidates from which to choose. In a secret ballot the Democrats cast their votes for one candidate for the position. If no candidate for the position receives a majority of the votes, as often is the case, the person who finished last in the balloting is removed from the list. There is then a second balloting held. This process continues through multiple ballots until one candidate is able to amass majority—50 percent plus one—support. In this way, supporters of losing candidates can reallocate their support to one of the remaining candidates who may be their second choice. This ensures the party that the winner of the leadership position is someone with wide support among the members and that no one can win with only a small plurality of the vote.

One variant of the Hare method is used in a few countries in conducting elections to political office. In these public elections, there is not multiple balloting, as in the U.S. House and many other organizations. Instead, voters list their complete order of preferences, as was done in the example of the Paradox of Voting above. The first-place preferences of the voters are tallied first. If, for example, there are five candidates in the election and no candidate gets a majority of the first-place votes, then the person with the fewest first-place votes is removed from the competition and his supporters' second-place preferences are allocated to the remaining four candidates. This process (removing last place finishers and allocating their supporters' next preferences to the remaining candidates) continues until one candidate receives majority support. An example of the Hare method in action is provided in the next section, entitled "Voting Method Alternatives."

The U.S. *run-off primary*, used mostly in southeastern states, is a form of Hare voting quite like the leadership race in the House. In it, if no candidate reaches some threshold (usually either 40 percent or 50 percent) in the first primary, then all but the top two candidates are eliminated for the second primary. The winner of the resulting two-candidate election becomes the nominee of the party.

There have been various other ways devised of taking into account the complete range of preferences of voters in elections. The methods described here are all in use in organizational and political elections around the world. One of these is called the *Borda count*. In it, points are awarded in descending order of the preference ordering of the voter.

In the United States, sports fans are well-acquainted with this sort of electoral procedure. The procedure is much like what is done in the Top Twenty polls used by news services to rate college sports teams. In it, the expert rates the teams one to twenty. The team rated first in the poll might receive twenty points, the number 2 team nineteen points, eighteen for number 3, on down the list. Points are tallied for all receiving votes. The team with the most points is the number 1 team in the country. Many organizations conduct elections for leadership positions or choose among policy options using the Borda count.

Another way commonly used to gauge more than just the first choice of the voters is called *approval voting*. It is the favorite of many academics for use in primary elections and many organizations for use in leadership elections, in part because of its relative simplicity. With approval voting voters are not required to make a comprehensive listing of their order of preference among the candidates. Instead, they are permitted to vote for all candidates of whom they approve. Voters do not make distinctions among the candidates they approve of. All approval votes cast carry equal weight. The winner of the election is the one receiving the most approval votes.

There are several alternative methods of tallying voters' preferences. Each is used either in organizational or political voting. Each has virtues and drawbacks. Below, for easy reference and summary, is a list and description of the methods and the purpose of each.

Voting Method Alternatives

Single-vote method: Each voter may cast a vote for only one candidate. Candidate with the most votes wins. This method of tallying votes aims to identify the candidate with the most first-choice support.

Runoff: If no candidate (using single-vote) gets a majority of votes in the first election, then another election is held between the top two finishers. The aim is to ensure that the ultimate winner of the election has broad support, and is not just the favorite of a committed plurality that supported the winner of the first election.

Hare method: Voters list all the candidates in order of preference (a *full preference ordering*). The first-place votes are tallied initially. If no candidate receives a majority of first-place votes, then the last-place finisher is eliminated, and his supporters' second-place votes are distributed among the survivors. This process is repeated (elimination of last-place finishers and redistribution of their support) until there is a candidate with majority support. This process offers advantages similar to the run-off method. It, however, eliminates lower finishers one by one, ensuring the identification of a winner who is not the favorite of only a small plurality.

Borda count: Voters make a complete preference ordering. In, for example, a four-candidate race, the candidates would receive three points for a first-place vote, two points for a second-place vote, one point for a third-place vote, and no points for a last-place vote. The candidate with the most points wins. This method takes into account in the final vote tally the complete preference ordering of all the voters.

Approval voting: Voters may cast votes for all candidates they approve of. No order of preference is given. The candidate with the most votes wins. This method offers a different and simpler way of ensuring that a candidate with the support of only a committed minority of voters cannot win an election.

Different Voting Methods: Which One is Best?

As the range of possibilities for counting votes or aggregating the preferences of the public in multicandidate elections becomes clear, the question arises: What difference does it make which method is used in an election? The following examples illustrate some of the issues that are raised by the use of different methods of voting and show exactly how the different methods work in practice.

Consider a population of twenty-one well-informed voters who provide their true preferences (no strategic voting) in an election. Their preference orderings in an election involving four candidates (A,B,C,D) as follows:

	$\underline{1}$	$\underline{2}$	$\underline{3}$	$\underline{4}$
V(1 - 7)	A	C	B	D
V(8 - 13)	C	B	D	A
V(14 - 18)	D	B	C	A
V(19 - 21)	B	D	C	A

The results of an election using the five methods of tallying votes listed and described above will include:

Using *Single-Vote Method:*

    A - 7 votes
    C - 6 votes
    D - 5 votes
    B - 3 votes

    A is declared the winner with the rules used in single-vote elections.

Using *Run Off Method:*

    The top two finishers qualify for the run-off election. They are A and C. This leaves D and B supporters free in the second primary to choose between A and C. According to their preference orderings, supporters of D and B would choose C over A. The runoff results are:

    C - 14 votes
    A - 7 votes

    C is declared the winner of the run off election.

Using *Hare Method:*

    With the Hare method, candidate B is eliminated after the tallying of first-choice preferences. B's supporters' second choice is D. These votes get redistributed accordingly. The second tallying of votes results in the following:

D - 8 votes
A - 7 votes
C - 6 votes

In this tallying, there is still no majority winner, so the last-place finisher, C, is eliminated. C voters get redistributed according to their next choice among remaining candidates. The results are:

D - 14 votes
A - 7 votes

There is finally a winner. D gets majority support.

Using *Borda Count Method:*

Going back to the full expression of voters' preferences the tally is as follows:

A receives 7 first-place votes at three points apiece; 14 last-place votes at no points apiece
B receives 3 first-place votes at three points apiece; 11 second-place votes at two points apiece; 7 third-place votes at one point apiece
C receives 6 first-place votes at three points apiece; 7 second-place votes at two points apiece; 8 third-place votes at one point apiece
D receives 5 first-place votes at three points apiece; 3 second-place votes at two points apiece; 6 third-place votes at one point apiece; 7 last-place votes at no points apiece

Results:

C - 40 points
B - 38 points
D - 27 points
A - 21 points

C wins with the most points.

Using *Approval Voting Method:*

For purposes of simplification, all voters are assumed to approve of their top two preferences. Based on that assumption, the results are as follows:

A receives 7 approval votes
B receives 14 approval votes
C receives 13 approval votes
D receives 8 approval votes

B wins the election having gained the most general approval by voters.

The above examples provide some curious results. To summarize:

Single Vote Winner: A
Runoff Winner: C
Hare Method Winner: D
Borda Winner: C
Approval Winner: B

The method most commonly used in the United States is, of course, the single vote. The use of this method identified A as the winner. Candidate A won with no other method, managing to make the runoff and the final Hare round before getting defeated rather easily by two different candidates, C and D. A came in a distant last place with both Borda and approval.

Different organizations and countries use different electoral methods, usually from among those described and used here, and there seems to be no obvious particularly good reason to choose one method over another. The only one that seems to be clearly inferior in this example is single-vote, which had a winner who did not come close to winning with any other method. Single-vote is the only one of these methods that considers only first choices of voters.

It is rather disturbing that the outcome of a democratically held election such as the one set up here *depends entirely on the way that the votes are tabulated!* Many times, of course, a great deal rides on the outcomes of elections. Note that these examples assumed that no voters acted strategically to try to manipulate the outcome. These were the honest preferences of the voters. It is simply not clear who should win. The sense that the outcomes of democratic elections should be fair representations of voters' preferences seems not to square with reality. Rather it seems that the outcome depends just as much on how votes are tallied as it does on what voters' preferences are. Strategic voting can alter the outcome of an election; how preferences are tallied also can determine election results.

Which of those candidates deserves to win that election? Is it too close to call? Which method identifies the candidate who actually *should* win?

Democratic elections, if held fairly, should identify the candidate most preferred by the voters. Which candidate is most preferred? Is there some way to assess which method is the best?

The Condorcet Winner

The above demonstration seems to lead to no clear and definitive solution. The peculiar quality of multicandidate elections is that there is not a self-evident answer to the question of who should win. The only conclusion that can be drawn from that example is hard for many people to swallow: In multicandidate elections there is no universally agreed upon method that is best to identify a winner. Some of the methods described, it can be argued, are better than others, but none is perfect. It is rather sobering to realize that the outcomes of elections with more than two candidates—including many primaries and elections in the United States (even many presidential elections, such as the 1992 presidential election with Bush, Perot, and Clinton)—may in fact be *arbitrary,* contingent on the method used to aggregate voters' preferences.

Fortunately there is one fairly simple and generally, if not universally, agreed upon criterion by which to judge methods of counting preferences and votes in multicandidate elections. It is something called the *Condorcet criterion.* The Condorcet criterion is simply a way to take literally the idea stressed before: that it is a reasonable objective to want the winner of an election to be the most preferred candidate. A reasonable definition of the most preferred candidate, according to scholars of social choice theory, is *the candidate who can beat all other candidates in one-to-one competition.* The candidate who can do that is literally preferred to all the others.

To determine which candidate is the Condorcet winner, it is necessary to have the full information about voter preferences provided in the last scenario and repeated here:

	$\underline{1}$	$\underline{2}$	$\underline{3}$	$\underline{4}$
V(1 - 7)	A	C	B	D
V(8 - 13)	C	B	D	A
V(14 - 18)	D	B	C	A
V(19 - 21)	B	D	C	A

Now it is possible to consider which candidate can beat all the others in pairwise comparisons. Below are all possible combinations of one-to-one matchups. The idea is that all voters are forced to consider their favorite in the pairwise match.

A v. B–B wins 14-7
A v. C–C wins 14-7
A v. D–D wins 14-7
B v. C–C wins 13-8
B v. D–B wins 16-5
C v. D–C wins 13-8

These results show that C is preferred to all the other candidates. C wins pairwise matchups with A, B, and D and is the Condorcet winner. The decision of this population can be depicted as follows:

C > B > D > A
(C defeats B, who defeats D, who defeats A—no candidate can
    defeat C)

C should be the winner in this election. Of course, C did not win with single-vote, Hare, or approval voting. A reform-minded person might ask why some method of counting votes similar to what we just performed in the above example is not employed in multicandidate elections. This method was able easily to identify the Condorcet winner, in a way that some of the methods of voting could not.

One answer is that there is not always a Condorcet winner. A significant fraction of the time in multicandidate elections, according to computer simulations, there would be no candidate who could beat all others in pairwise comparisons. (Merrill [1988, 20] suggests that in a five-candidate race there might not be a Condorcet winner about a fifth of the time, although this percentage could vary depending on a large number of variables.) Reconsider the Paradox of Voting looked at earlier (sometimes called a *cycle*). A cycle occurs when there is no Condorcet winner.

Such a cycle could be produced easily with only a slight alteration of the set of preferences used above. Consider what the results of a method designed to identify the Condorcet winner would be were voters 14-18 to reverse their ratings of candidates C and A, such that these five voters rated D first and B second, as before, but placed A ahead of C.

Instead of: C > B > D > A, as shown above, the result would
    be: C > B > D > A > C

This is because, in a pairwise comparison of A and C, A is now preferred by twelve voters, to C being preferred by only nine. So while A loses out to both B and D, it can beat C.

So, since in a significant fraction of elections a population would not have a most preferred candidate or Condorcet winner, then the Condorcet method is not very useful as an electoral procedure. Other voting methods only fail to identify a winner in the tiny probability of there being a tie. Use of some sort of Condorcet method would result frequently in no winner being identified. The other methods all at least have the virtue of almost always producing a winner by generally agreed upon rules.

But the concept of a Condorcet winner is not a useless one, even though the Condorcet method of aggregating voters' preferences is not very useful. It still would be beneficial to have an electoral procedure that as often as possible identified the Condorcet winner when there was one. It is instructive to look back at the example of the various electoral procedures in use. In that example, some of the procedures identified C (the Condorcet winner) as the winner, and some did not: the runoff and the Borda count identified the Condorcet winner, and approval, Hare, and single-vote did not. In other words, in this case Borda and runoff worked. But this is only one example. It would be interesting to know which procedures identify the Condorcet winner *with the most regularity.*

The concept of computing the *Condorcet efficiency* of electoral systems, applied to elections by mathematician Samuel Merrill, aims to do exactly that. Condorcet efficiency is the percentage of the time a method of voting identifies the Condorcet winner, when there is a Condorcet winner. Merrill, with the aid of computer simulations using various assumptions about the ideological distributions of the voters and the ideological distribution of the candidates relative to the voters, has rated the Condorcet efficiency of the voting methods described here.

It is not important here to get into the details about the various assumptions that Merrill made. It should be pointed out that Condorcet efficiency can vary a great deal, depending on the assumptions made, but there are certain regularities that are almost unvarying. Central among them is the fact that, no matter what assumptions are made, single-vote does worse than other methods, usually quite a bit worse. Table 5.1 shows the typical findings in the simulations.

As can be seen from the chart, different methods of voting have substantially varying Condorcet efficiency. It would be desirable to use a method of voting and tallying votes that would identify the Condorcet winner as often as possible. The disturbing result is that the Condorcet efficiency of the method in common use in the United States, single-vote, is consistently the lowest, especially when the number of candidates competing exceeds three. All of the other options have a superior tendency to identify the Condorcet winner when the field of candidates is large. Borda is regularly seen to have the best efficiency. Hare, in different simulations, can be as good as Borda or almost as weak as single-vote. Approval usually is much better than single-vote, often similar to Hare, and a bit worse than Borda. It should be noted that, under some circumstances, the Condorcet efficiency of single-vote is *much* lower than shown in table 5.1. In some simulations, with five candidates in the running, its efficiency can be as low as 20-25 percent. It seems the use of single-vote is misguided in some circumstances—such as when the field of candidates competing is large. In view of this sort of analysis its use should be reconsidered under some conditions.

It is not the case, however, that all methods of voting are feasible or appropriate for all types of elections. The remainder of this section evaluates the appropriateness of the various voting systems for presidential primaries, taking into account Condorcet efficiency and other relevant considerations.

Table 5.1
Approximate Condorcet Efficiency of different voting systems*

	Number of Candidates			
	2	3	4	5
Single-vote	100	78	69	57
Hare	100	95	88	78
Approval	100	86	78	77
Borda	100	92	88	87

* Merrill ran numerous computer simulations to gauge the Condorcet efficiency of different voting systems. He changed some of the variables, including the way that the voters' preferences were distributed on an ideological spectrum, and how candidates were distributed relative to the voters. In this case, I have made approximations based on Merrill's results with the candidates and the voters distributed similarly along an ideological spectrum.

Condorcet efficiency can vary a good deal depending on the assumptions made. In most of the simulations conducted by Merrill, Hare, approval, and Borda remain far superior to single-vote. Single-vote frequently dips below 50 percent Condorcet efficiency, depending on the assumptions, when there are five or more candidates running.

Source: Samuel Merrill (1988), *Making Multicandidate Elections More Democratic*

Single-Vote: The major drawback of single-vote is its relative, and really disturbing, tendency not to award victory (or the most delegates in the case of a presidential primary) to the Condorcet winner. This is particularly true when the field of candidates exceeds three, as frequently is the case in the early events in Iowa, New Hampshire, and other states.

The events that take place in these early states in presidential nomination campaigns are of singular importance. While the outcomes of these small early states do not determine the parties' nominees, they do provide early momentum for successful candidates, and they serve to eliminate many candidates who do poorly. Of course, these results are interpreted on the basis of a single-vote aggregation of preferences; this method of aggregation does not seem always to depict well the true preferences of the public.

Single-vote has the advantage of being easy for voters to understand and easy for vote counters to deal with. These advantages are substantial; the very legitimacy of electoral procedures depends in part on the public's understanding and acceptance of those procedures.

Runoff: The runoff is not realistic or relevant for presidential primaries. While the runoff is in common use in primaries for other offices in which the determination of the final winner is made, in presidential primaries the contest moves quickly on to other states, and it is not crucial to determine the final winner. It is, however, crucial to allot delegates in a way consistent with the expressed preferences of the voters.

Hare: In the above example the Hare method did not identify the Condorcet winner, but all studies, including Merrill's computer simulations, arrive at the finding that Hare is far better at identifying the most preferred candidate on a regular basis than single-vote. Hare could be adapted to presidential primaries by using it to identify the winning candidate, then allotting the state's delegates on the basis of the final result.

The most compelling criticism of Hare is that it asks too much of voters. Methods that require complete listings of preferences, some argue, are useful only for elections in smaller organizations in which the participants all are likely to be fully informed. In a public election in a democracy, some maintain that it is not realistic to use methods that require this level of information of the voters. Merrill argues: "Simplicity of a procedure . . . helps voters understand and respect the outcome" (Merrill 1988, 107).

Borda: The same criticism leveled at Hare can be leveled at Borda. It too requires a complete listing of preferences. Borda has another, perhaps more damaging, drawback. The listing of preferences in Borda is susceptible to a pernicious form of strategic voting.

Strategic voting (not expressing your true preferences in order to enhance the chances of either your first choice winning or a less preferred candidate losing) is not necessarily a controversial or pernicious act. With single-vote, if a voter's first choice has no chance of winning in his or her view, it makes perfect sense and seems to square with most notions of fairness to cast the vote for a second choice. But with Borda, a voter's entire preference ranking has an impact on the outcome. A voter has the opportunity not just to reward his or her second choice with a number one ranking because the candidate seems more viable than one's first choice, but also to *punish* a less preferred candidate. If, in a five-candidate race (A, B, C, D, E), the two top contenders in the polls, A and B, are also a voter's top two preferences (A first, B second), there might be an incentive with Borda for the voter to punish B by ranking B last, so that he gets no points.

Note that with the other method that requires a complete listing, Hare, there is no such incentive to punish a second-choice candidate by placing him last.

This is because, with Hare, a voter's second, third, fourth, and further preferences are not taken into consideration until his or her first choice is eliminated.

Suffice it to say that if someone finds merit in a method with complete preference listings, Hare is better than Borda. Hare encourages voters to provide honest preference listings and does not encourage the punitive type of strategic voting that Borda does.

Approval: Approval seems to combine some of the better characteristics of Hare and single-vote. Approval has the benefit of a strong Condorcet efficiency rating, far superior to single-vote. (It is, however, somewhat weaker in this category than Borda.) It also has the benefit of being simple for voters and vote counters.

No complete preference listing is required, but some sense is gleaned about voters' second and other preferences by allowing them to vote for all candidates they approve of. Of course, approval is susceptible to a kind of strategic voting in which a voter might only vote for his or her first choice, and not for other candidates of whom he or she approves, in order not to spread support to competitors. But this sort of strategic voting is in no way comparable to the kind that may occur with Borda. With Borda a voter has the opportunity to weaken a rival candidate vis-à-vis other candidates. With approval, this kind of action cannot be taken by a voter.

There are several important points that should be stressed at this point in this short course on public choice in multicandidate elections. The most important lessons are:

1. With any electoral procedure, mistakes will be made. No method guarantees the identification of the Condorcet winner.

2. There is a significant percentage of elections in which there will be no Condorcet winner. It is impossible to know for sure when this occurs, but when it does, the identification of a winner is arbitrary, dependent on the type of voting used.

3. Some electoral procedures are better than others in the regularity with which they identify Condorcet winners.

4. The regularity with which methods of voting identify Condorcet winners is heavily dependent on the number of candidates competing. Some methods of voting become badly inefficient as the number of candidates competing increases.

The sort of arbitrariness *inherent* in multicandidate elections may be a difficult concept for some people to accept, but it is truly a fact of life in democratic politics. Electoral procedures are better or worse, but none is perfect or fair all the time. The best that can be done is to use a method that enhances Condorcet efficiency while at the same time offering voters a way to participate with full understanding of the consequences of their participation.

In summary, single-vote is a highly problematical method of voting. It is simple, a virtue, but it only regularly identifies the Condorcet winner when three (or of course two) candidates are running. Borda wins the contest for best Condorcet efficiency; Hare also does quite well. But both methods require a complete preference ordering. This, together with the complex method of tabulation used, may make it so citizens are not fully knowledgeable of the consequences of their participation. (Also, it is surely an open question whether anything approaching reasonable distinctions can be made by most voters on a long list of candidates.) Borda carries with it all the freight of Hare (complexity for voters) and is susceptible to a punitive form of strategic voting. Approval combines some good qualities of single-vote (relative simplicity) and Hare (improved Condorcet efficiency as compared to single-vote).

The next section looks at precisely how the preceding primer on social choice theory is relevant to presidential primaries.

Condorcet and Presidential Primaries

In one important way, a presidential primary differs from other multicandidate races in primaries or general elections. In a primary for an office other than president, the first-place finisher (except in run-off states) is the nominee, the winner. In general elections, the same holds true. The outcome is unambiguous. (Although it should be pointed out that the failure of single-vote to identify the most preferred candidate in many of these elections is a persistent drawback.) Presidential primaries are different in that any one primary does not determine the nominee. In short, the results of presidential primaries are used to determine the allotment of delegates, not immediately and finally the winner of the nomination.

Of course, it still would be desirable to have the allotment of delegates based on an accurate and fair reflection of the voters' preferences. On the Republican side this is particularly important since the allotment of delegates is made on a winner-take-all basis in many states. Consider that the second-place finisher in a Republican primary may get few or no delegates but may very well be the most preferred candidate. The same may go for the third-place finisher. It is potentially the case in Republican primary states that someone other than the Condorcet winner will receive *all* of the delegates.

On the Democratic side, the problem of the failure to identify the Condorcet winner is mitigated a little by the use of proportional allocation of delegates. A Condorcet winner finishing somewhere other than first is very likely at least to pick up some delegate support in a state. The stakes are not quite so large in any one primary as they are on the GOP side in many states.

But there are reasons other than the fairness of the allotment of delegates to be concerned about the issue of identifying the Condorcet winner in presidential primaries. These are further ramifications of using single-vote, with all its weaknesses, in the peculiar process the parties use to nominate presidential candidates.

In presidential nomination politics, primaries are spread over about three and a half months in the spring of the presidential election year. Few of the candidates running in any given year have the resources to stay in the race throughout the period of the primaries without the free publicity by the major media and infusion of contributions that come with winning early primaries. The point is that a first-place finish often is *far* more important than the number of delegates that get allotted to a particular candidate; a finish other than first may doom a candidacy, regardless of the number of delegates secured.

Iowa, New Hampshire, and other early states involve very few delegates. But most candidacies fail to remain viable after only the first few small state primaries and caucuses. A first-place finish may be absolutely critical to the success of a candidacy. A good showing in these states can make or break a candidacy. Oddly enough, with the large numbers of candidates receiving votes in these states in most elections years (with, of course, the single-vote method of voting), it is probably common that the most preferred candidate is *not* the first-place finisher. There is a great deal riding on the outcomes of these states above and beyond delegates; at the same time there is good reason to be very skeptical about the nature of the results using single-vote.

The concept of *momentum*, as described by Bartels and others (covered in chapter 3 in considerable depth), is relevant in considering the value of early first-place finishers. Candidates such as Bush in 1980, Hart in 1984, and Tsongas in 1992 gathered support nationally because of first-place finishes in early states. These were all plurality victories, in which there was no certainty that these men were actually the Condorcet winners. Momentum usually is generated based on early state victories, tremendously exaggerating the importance of these states relative to the amount of delegates available to be won in them.

This sort of public choice analysis has a clear lesson for the study of presidential nomination campaigns. What is happening is that candidacies are often made or broken based on analytically questionable outcomes from early state primaries, because of the importance placed on these states. The outcomes from these states often may be inconclusive from a public choice standpoint (if there is no Condorcet winner), and it likely is common that when there is a Condorcet winner he is not the one awarded with the bonanza of publicity for a first place-finish. Chapter 6 delves more into the implications of these lessons.

Other Criteria of Fairness

Only one criterion associated with a fair electoral procedure—the Condorcet criterion—has been examined so far. For many simple electoral procedures, such as a primary for a lower office or a general election, it is the most important and relevant fairness criterion. But presidential nomination procedures are nothing if not complex electoral procedures. The *serialization* of electoral events—having a series of primaries and precinct caucuses over the course of three and a half months—makes this procedure unique, as does the fact that the field of candidates changes over the course of the campaign. Furthermore, delegate allocation is done in Byzantine fashion in most states. As was suggested in chapter 1, this may be the most peculiar, most loosely organized, and most complex public process of selecting a candidate ever devised by man.

For these reasons, the question of fairness in this process of public choice requires more than just the consideration of the Condorcet criterion. Public choice methodologists, ever since the modern father of public choice analysis Kenneth Arrow, have developed other criteria for determining the fairness of electoral procedures. William Riker (1982) devised the generally accepted list of such criteria that are useful in assessing the weaknesses of any method of public choice. Included in this list, of course, is the Condorcet criterion:

Condorcet Criterion: If a candidate beats or ties all others in pairwise comparisons, then that candidate should be the winner.

The other criteria are as follows:

Undifferentiatedness: Shifting the preference orders among the voters should not change the outcome. In other words, the identity of the voters should have no effect on the outcome.

Neutrality: No candidate should have a favored position in the voting system.

Monotonicity: A higher judgment on a winning candidate by some voter or voters should not make that candidate lose; a lower judgment on a losing candidate should not cause that candidate to win.

Consistency: If the electorate is divided into parts for election purposes, and one candidate wins or ties in all parts, then that candidate should be the winner of the whole.

Independence From Irrelevant Alternatives: The same outcome should result from the same profile of ordinal preferences (Riker 1982, 99-101).

While the precise meaning of these criteria may not immediately be clear, all the criteria turn out to be commonsensical standards of fairness. Of course, presidential primaries (or any multicandidate election) can violate the Condorcet criterion. What is interesting is that the presidential nomination process potentially violates *all* of the criteria developed by Riker—as the next chapter demonstrates. For now, the notions of fairness represented by these five new criteria are described in plain language below.

The concept of *undifferentiatedness* is no different from the democratic principle of one person-one vote. Basically, everyone's vote should have the same impact on the outcome. *Undifferentiatedness*, in the language of social choice theory, simply says that it should not matter to the outcome of an electoral procedure which person has which preference ordering, since all persons should be equal in democratic electoral procedures.

Neutrality applies to candidates what undifferentiatedness applies to voters. Essentially, no candidate should have a favored or advantaged position in a fair electoral system. The electoral landscape should be fair; stated colloquially, that the playing field should be level.

Monotonicity, while also logical in terms of fairness, is a more abstract criterion than undifferentiatedness or neutrality. In view of the full ordering of preferences by voters, it makes sense that improving the ranking of a candidate in one or more voter's preference ordering should not cause that candidate to *lose*. Similarly, lowering the ranking of a candidate in one or more voter's preference ordering should not cause that candidate to *win*. This criterion seems impossible to violate, but violation of it is indeed possible in presidential nomination campaigns (see chapter 6).

The *consistency* criterion says that a candidate who wins or ties in all parts of an electorate that has been divided for the purpose of an election, should win that election. This also may seem impossible to violate. In the next chapter we will see how the presidential nomination process can violate it.

The *independence from irrelevant alternatives* criterion states, in effect, that as long as the *relative* position of the candidates in the preference ordering of all the voters stays the same, the outcome should remain the same. In effect, the addition or subtraction of candidates who cannot, in any eventuality, win should not alter the outcome of the election.

Conclusion

This primer on social choice theory, has shown how any election involving more than two candidates is subject to doubt and criticism as to the fairness of its outcome. Different methods of aggregating voters' preferences can result in different outcomes of elections, and the most preferred candidate, the Condorcet winner, may not be identified always by any of the electoral procedures commonly in use. Not only that, there may not even be a Condorcet winner. What is particularly startling is that the most commonly used method of aggregating voters' preferences is the one least likely to identify the most preferred candidate.

This chapter developed a set of criteria, some of which are self-evident in a democracy (one person-one vote), others of which are considerably more abstract, to assess electoral procedures. This set of criteria is very useful for analyzing the relative merit of different electoral procedures, as well as for identifying the weaknesses in the procedures. Chapter 6 will use this set of criteria to evaluate the presidential nomination process.

Chapter Six

Assessing Presidential Primaries as a Method of Public Choice

It is only in recent years that scholars have acknowledged the trends in presidential nomination campaigns that have made them into plebiscitary events. Increasingly, students of presidential campaigns and presidential politics have been treating these nomination campaigns—as they should—as election campaigns instead of extended efforts by potential contenders to curry the favor of party leaders for the purpose of securing delegates votes at a representative convention. Voting behavior in presidential primaries is finally getting subjected to the kind of scrutiny that congressional races, gubernatorial races, and general elections for president have for decades. Similarly, scholars of the impact of the mass media and advertising in political campaigns have begun focusing on the presidential nomination races in the ways that they always have focused on other election campaigns.

John Aldrich, Steven Brams, Paul Gurian, and others (see chapter 3) have pioneered the intensive study of the dynamics of presidential nomination campaigns. (Even the existence of strategic voting in presidential primaries, alluded to in chapter 5, has been the subject of empirical analysis [Abramson et al. 1992].) Much of this scholarly attention, most of it since about 1980, was brought together and supplemented with original findings by Larry Bartels in his seminal work, *Presidential Primaries and the Dynamics of Public Choice*, in 1988.

Bartels's work has spawned numerous subsequent studies on the dynamics of the nomination campaigns. Still, little work has been done in subjecting the electoral procedures of the nomination process to a rigorous analysis based on the analytical tools of social choice theory introduced in chapter 5.

The electoral arrangements in presidential nomination campaigns are certainly peculiar. There are three characteristics in particular that distinguish these campaigns from most others.

1. No other electoral process features an unpredictably changing field of candidates over the course of the campaign.
2. Presidential nomination races feature a series of elections spread out over three and a half months with different electorates for each of the public events.
3. The methods by which the states translate and interpret the participants' votes vary a great deal.

Several questions come to mind when one views these sorts of arrangements as a method of public choice. How fair and democratic, from the standpoint of social choice theory, is such an electoral arrangement? If it is unfair, in what ways can it be improved to make it more fair? Is it fairer from a strict public choice standpoint than potential alternative arrangements?

These three questions are addressed in chapters 7 and 8. This chapter examines just how unfair the current arrangements are when put under the microscope of social choice theory. Chapter 7 compares the current process with the alternatives (national primary, convention/national primary, regional primaries) that were introduced in chapter 4.

Analysis

The first step in this analysis is to establish what can be accomplished by subjecting an electoral arrangement to the criteria of fairness devised by William Riker (and first introduced in chapter 5). No electoral process involving more than two candidates can be perfectly fair, since all elections with more than two candidates always have the potential to violate the Condorcet criterion. As such, when electoral procedures are compared (for example, the national primary against the current process, as chapter 7 does) by the standards of the fairness criteria, the terms of debate are limited to the degree to which different procedures violate these principles of fairness. These criteria are of considerable heuristic value in revealing how fair and democratic the electoral arrangements are. But these criteria say nothing about the other aspects of a good campaign environment—such as whether voters are learning about the candidates and candidates about the voters, or whether voters are forced to live with hastily made decisions, or whether potentially good candidates are discouraged from running. The social choice criteria are only one part of assessing and comparing alternative electoral arrangements.

This section shows how it is possible that all six criteria of fairness can be violated in a nomination campaign arranged as the current one is. For each of the fairness criteria that are reproduced below, there is a precise description of how the current nomination process can violate the fairness principle involved. Following that is a look at some of the implications the fairness (or lack of fairness) of the process have for presidential nomination politics. Specifically, there are two critical problems with the structure of the nomination process that relate directly to violations of three of the criteria.

Riker's criteria are summarized below.

Undifferentiatedness: Permuting preference orders among voters should not change the outcome. The identity of the voters should have no effect on the outcome.

Neutrality : No alternative should have a favored position in the voting system.

Monotonicity: A higher judgment on a winning alternative should not make it lose; a lower judgment on a loser should not make it win.

Condorcet Criterion: If an alternative beats or ties all others in pairwise comparisons, then it ought to win.

Consistency: If the electorate is divided into parts for election purposes and if one alternative wins or ties in all parts, then it ought to be chosen in the whole.

Independence from Irrelevant Alternatives: The same outcome should result from the same profile of ordinal preferences. (Riker 1982, 99-101)

Undifferentiatedness

Obviously no sensible person would *plan* or intend to have an electoral procedure that violated the principle of one person-one vote, unless there was some extremely compelling reason to do so. In fact, however, in the presidential nomination process, voters in some states, year in and year out, have far more impact on the outcome of the race than those in other states.

It has been a regular occurrence that states that hold their primaries later in the campaign are asking for the voters' preferences long after the nomination is a foregone conclusion. Furthermore, these later states seem always to have less of an impact on the winnowing of the field of candidates than states holding their primaries at the beginning of the delegate selection phase of the nomination process. If any sense of democratic fairness in the nomination process is to be obtained, there surely needs to be some good reasons to have an arrangement that potentially violates one person-one vote principle.

It should be noted that it has been the case in several of the nomination campaigns in recent years that states holding primaries later in the delegate selection phase have had an important influence on the selection of a party's nominee, albeit a different sort of influence from the early states. On the Democratic side in 1984, voters in later states made the ultimately determinative choice among Walter Mondale, Gary Hart, and Jesse Jackson. Similarly, in 1988 Democratic primary voters in later states made the determination in the winnowed field of candidates between survivors Michael Dukakis and Jesse Jackson. The same could be said of voters in later states in choosing Bill Clinton over Jerry Brown in the 1992 Democratic campaign.

In republican contests in 1988 and 1980, however, voters in later states were left with a field of one candidate, George Bush and Ronald Reagan, respectively. In the 1980 Democratic race, while voters in later states were presented with a choice of Edward Kennedy and Jimmy Carter, Carter actually had to borrow a phrase from many baseball division pennant races, mathematically eliminated Kennedy. Given the proportional rules governing delegate allocation on the Democratic side, Carter had, for all intents and purposes, built up an insurmountable lead by the later stages of the public phase of the campaign.

It is significant that voters in later states can make decisive determinations, but often they are not in a position to do so, their participation at that point rendered essentially meaningless. And early states always play a crucial role in determining which candidates will be weeded out. It cannot be said that any one state's voters determine the nominee of one of the parties but it is the case that voters in states such as Iowa and New Hampshire have a disproportionate impact in determining which candidates maintain viability.

It is no mystery as to what causes this *differentiatedness* in the nomination process, that is, the violation of one person-one vote. It is the serialization of caucuses and primaries that produces the violation of this principle. The dynamics of a serialized process (which works to winnow the field of candidates as early as the first of March) have resulted in a great impact on the campaign for some of the early states and often in no role at all for the voters in states falling later in the calendar.

Doing away with the unfairness caused by differentiatedness can only be done with a one-day national primary. The national primary has been criticized on numerous grounds, and chapter 7 makes a systematic comparison of the two processes. Suffice it to say for now that the national primary is criticized for its contribution to the further atrophy of the party system, the end of the salutary effects of retail politicking in smaller states, the tremendous expense involved for candidates to compete in a national primary compared to the relatively low "start-up costs" of Iowa and New Hampshire, and the impediment for little-known candidates to develop and gain attention.

For the time being if a national primary is deemed undesirable for these or other reasons, *differentiatedness is inevitable* within any sort of plebiscitary framework that places primaries and precinct caucuses in some sort of sequential ordering in presidential nomination campaigns. A violation of the one person-one vote principle of the sort described here would exist whether something resembling the current schedule of state primaries continues to be used or, as many have suggested is desirable, a set of regional primaries were instituted.

To summarize, the serialization of primaries is what causes the differentiatedness. At the same time, serialization is what allows the process to have retail campaigning instead of exclusively large-scale media campaigning. Because of this and other advantages, serialization is an aspect of this peculiar method of public choice that is defended by many as desirable. At this stage, the use of serialized primaries in any form necessarily violates a bedrock principle of democratic fairness.

Neutrality

The current nomination process does not have a level playing field when viewed from the standpoint of social choice theory. Of course, there are many ways in which any election could be said not to have a level playing field. One obvious example from nearly all elections held in the United States is that it is extremely rare that the candidates competing have equal financial resources. But this strictly analytical discussion will ignore that sort of potential unfairness. Instead, it deals with questions of the fairness of the electoral arrangements and the way that voters' preferences are aggregated and counted.

In presidential nomination politics there are two ways that the principle of neutral electoral arrangements is violated.

First, it is easily conceivable that rearranging the order of the states' primaries could alter the outcome of a particular campaign. The reason is simple. The apparently inexorable dynamics of the serialized presidential primaries and precinct caucuses force most of the candidates to the sidelines based on poor performances in early events. Is it possible that were Tennessee and Arizona (for example) to hold their primaries first instead of Iowa and New Hampshire, the candidates who would survive and who would be eliminated might differ?

There are good reasons to think so. The main reason is that, however measured, voters in different states surely have different political predispositions and would be inclined to give different levels of support to the various candidates in a party in any given nomination campaign (Bartels 1988; Parent, Jillson, and Weber 1987; Yu 1987). It is likely that different candidates would be eliminated from contention depending on which states started out the campaign. As such, the electoral process that puts Iowa and New Hampshire first systematically favors some candidates over others.

This last point does not necessarily lead to the conclusion that the leading or front-running candidates in past campaigns would have been eliminated if states other than Iowa and New Hampshire had started the process. But it is possible that the distinctive characteristics of the voters of those states might make a viable contender out of a candidate who might not do well were other states to start out the process.

As an issue of social choice theory, candidates who do not survive the early tests theoretically can be influential on the outcome of a nomination race. A specific example of this possibility is covered in the section on the Independence from Irrelevant Alternatives criterion. Weaker candidates who manage to stay alive because of strong performances in Iowa and New Hampshire can have an effect on the outcome of later primaries by taking away votes from one or another of the stronger candidates. In other words, if Iowa and New Hampshire tend to prop up or favor a certain type of candidate, as they might, this type of candidate can have an effect on the nomination race in later states that he might not otherwise have were other states to lead off the process.

It might be possible to scramble the order of the primaries from campaign to campaign to end the regular outsized influence of Iowa and New Hampshire. This would, however, only change the bias from election to election.

As with differentiatedness, the sort of non-neutrality described here is a result of the serialization of the primaries and precinct caucuses, and is in fact inevitable with serialization. The only remedy—the national primary—is considered in more detail in chapter 7.

Another violation of the principle of the neutrality of electoral arrangements has to do with the way delegate allocation is handled by the states in nomination campaigns. Rules of delegate selection and allocation vary from state to state and may prove to be unfair to certain candidates. It would be possible, for example, if rules varied from state to state, that one candidate could receive more votes in the primaries yet win fewer delegates than another candidate. For example, a candidate with particular strength in states with winner-take-all rules would have a built-in advantage in the contest to win delegates. This candidate could build up a large margin in the delegate count over his closest competitor, even if he only won these states by a small margin in the popular vote. His opponent might win states with proportional delegate allocation rules by larger margins but accumulate fewer delegates in the process, since losing candidates in states with those sorts of rules also can qualify for delegates to the national convention.

The potential for this sort of unfairness is far greater on the Republican side. In the GOP, states choose from a variety of methods of allocation, including winner-take-all, districted winner-take-all or bonus plans, and proportional allocation. The Republicans have never restricted the states as to the rules for delegate allocation, and some states actually make up the rules as they go along in the process of selecting delegates. In 1988 nearly half of the Republican state parties used some form of winner-take-all rules to allocate delegates based on the outcome of a plebiscitary event. Thus it is possible, in this environment, to win more popular votes than a competitor, as described in the last paragraph, but still not receive as many delegates as that competitor.

The Democrats have a more uniform method, with most Democratic state parties using proportional allocation by district. The problem with violating the neutrality criterion almost has been eliminated by the Democrats. They have lowered the threshold for receiving delegates from 20 percent of the popular vote to 15 percent, and they do not permit any rules other than proportional allocation of delegates.

The Democrats' rules, from the standpoint of the neutrality principle, are obviously fairer. But there is an important consequence of these rules that the Republicans may be said to benefit from. Weaker trial-balloon candidacies are more likely to fall to earth quickly with winner-take-all rules, having been allotted fewer delegates (or none at all) for finishing behind the winner. This enables the front-runner to consolidate a majority of delegates earlier in the race and avoid whatever deleterious effects more divisive primaries might have on the party's chances for victory in November (Lengle 1980, 1995). Although the evidence is anecdotal on this point, it is the case that in the two multicandidate GOP races in recent years (1980 and 1988), the eventual winner's competition was weeded out very early—by the time of the South Carolina primary in 1980 and on Super Tuesday in 1988.

On the Democratic side, more candidates have lasted longer in every multicandidate race (1976, 1984, 1988, and 1992). Although this difference between the parties may be at least in part the result of a different structure of factional competition within the two parties rather than just attributable to different rules for delegate allocation in the states, it is true that second- and third-place finishers make off with far more delegates on the Democratic side than on the Republican side, since many GOP state parties allot few or no delegates to losers. Presumably these trial-balloon Democrats can justify keeping their campaigns going longer as a result.

Yet it also should be noted that enough winnowing has happened on the Democratic side, even with the fairer rules, that a majority winner always has emerged during the primaries. Even proportional rules do not seem to keep enough candidacies viable long enough to keep the party from coalescing around a majority winner. The dynamics of multicandidate races described by Aldrich, Bartels, and others seem to apply irrespective of the differences in delegate allocation rules used by the two parties.

With regard to the second type of violation of neutrality, such unfairness can nearly be removed with the use of proportional allocation rules. However, even the fairer proportional allocation of delegates is troubled by a more profound difficulty: violations of the Condorcet criterion may render unfair any method of delegate allocation based on the popular vote.

Monotonicity

The presidential nomination process has two particularly crucial and distinguishing characteristics. First, delegate selection events occur sequentially. Second, some candidates, for a variety of reasons, are forced to drop out of the running after early events, usually because of poor performance, an occurrence that may change the field of candidates from event to event.

The following example is a simplified model of the presidential nomination campaign that incorporates these two characteristics. It illustrates how some of the dynamics of a serialized process can violate the monotonicity criterion.

In this example borrowed from Doron and Kronick (1977), there are four candidates, W, X, Y, and Z. There are two primaries held at different times, replicating the sequential nature of primaries in the real campaigns. For both primaries the distribution of preferences among the voters is identical, as depicted below. The dynamics of the process are reproduced by having the last-place finisher drop out after the first primary. The single-vote method of voting is used, as in real life.

	$\underline{1}$	$\underline{2}$	$\underline{3}$	$\underline{4}$
V(1 - 9)	W	Z	X	Y
V(10 - 15)	X	Y	Z	W
V(16 - 17)	Y	X	Z	W
V(18 - 21)	Y	Z	X	W
V(22 - 26)	Z	X	Y	W

In this situation, Z would drop out after the first primary because of receiving the fewest number of first-place votes. X would benefit from this development because X is the second choice of Z voters and would receive those votes in the second primary. X would actually win the second primary with the addition of the Z supporters. X would then have eleven votes, more than W's nine and Y's six.

Imagine that voters 16 and 17 changed their preference order from $Y > X > Z > W$ to $X > Y > Z > W$. The new scenario would look like this:

	$\underline{1}$	$\underline{2}$	$\underline{3}$	$\underline{4}$
V(1 - 9)	W	Z	X	Y
V(10 - 15)	X	Y	Z	W
V(16 - 17)	X	Y	Z	W
V(18 - 21)	Y	Z	X	W
V(22 - 26)	Z	X	Y	W

Note that this change constitutes an improvement in X's position. It also would cause Y to be the last-place finisher in the first primary and subsequently to drop out of the race. Y's support among voters 18 through 21 in the second primary would transfer to Z. Z then would have nine votes in the second primary, which would tie Z for first place. X's support in the second primary would be eight votes instead of eleven, causing X to finish in third place instead of first place in the second primary. In other words, an improvement of X's position among some of the voters (voters 16 and 17) works to X's disadvantage in the campaign. This is a violation of monotonicity.

This violation is an entirely theoretical one, in that voters 16 and 17 will, of course, decide for themselves how they will vote in the first primary, with the resulting resignation of whichever candidate comes in last. The monotonicity violation is still a useful tool in understanding some of the peculiarities of a campaign with sequential electoral events. The idea that an *improvement* in a candidate's performance theoretically can have a negative effect on that candidate's prospects in this sort of electoral arrangement is an interesting discovery.

Condorcet Criterion

In Chapter 5 we took a detailed look at the so-called Condorcet problem. Any election with more than two alternatives can violate the Condorcet criterion. In presidential nomination politics, the Condorcet criterion violation bears most directly on the issue of aggregating fairly the preferences of the voters. The violation also affects indirectly, although profoundly, the manner and fairness with which delegates are allocated. It may be in looking at the Condorcet criterion violation that the difficulties in using presidential primaries as a method of public choice come into clearest focus.

Samuel Merrill (1988) conducted a study of the rate at which different voting systems identify the Condorcet winner (Condorcet efficiency). That chart is reproduced in table 6.1.

Table 6.1
Approximate Condorcet Efficiency of different voting systems*

	Number of Candidates			
	2	3	4	5
Single-vote	100	78	69	57
Hare	100	95	88	78
Approval	100	86	78	77
Borda	100	92	88	87

* Merrill ran numerous computer simulations to gauge the Condorcet efficiency of different voting systems. He changed some of the variables, including the way that the voters' preferences were distributed on an ideological spectrum, and how candidates were distributed relative to the voters. In this case, I have made approximations based on Merrill's results with the candidates and the voters distributed similarly along an ideological spectrum.

Condorcet efficiency can vary a good deal depending on the assumptions made. In most of the simulations conducted by Merrill, Hare, approval, and Borda remain far superior to single-vote. Single-vote frequently dips below 50 percent Condorcet efficiency, depending on the assumptions, when there are five or more candidates running.

Source: Samuel Merrill (1988), *Making Multicandidate Elections More Democratic*

Single-vote, the method in use across the country in presidential primaries with large fields of candidates is particularly weak at identifying the Condorcet winner.

The question of Condorcet efficiency is very important when the problem of delegate allocation brought up in the second part of the discussion of the violations of neutrality is considered. It is rather obvious that a proportional allocation of delegates is fairer than winner-take-all, but if the allocation is done on the basis of a vote that does not accurately represent the preferences of the voters, the method of delegate allocation becomes rather secondary to the primary problem of a flawed method of counting votes.

Of course, it is better only to give a larger proportion of the delegates to an undeserving winner (under proportional rules) than to give that candidate all or nearly all of the delegates (as would be the case under some form of winner-take-all rules). But *any* allocation of delegates based on a voting system that is not regularly able to identify the Condorcet winner is problematic at best. From a fairness standpoint, what does it matter what method of delegate allocation is used if the results upon which the allocations are made do not very accurately reflect the preferences of the voting public?

It is probably the case in some campaigns for presidential nominations that the winner of one crucial primary or another (usually early in the campaign) is not the Condorcet winner. This undeserving candidate not only receives the most delegates (maybe nearly all of them) but also may enjoy the beneficial effects of the momentum generated on the basis of positive media attention from that early victory in subsequent primaries.

Many critics, Brams most assiduously (Brams and Fishburn 1983), have suggested the use of approval voting (voters may cast a vote for all candidates they approve of) in multicandidate primary elections. Approval voting does have a higher Condorcet efficiency than single-vote, as do some other voting methods. (Two of the other methods of voting that have been suggested are the Borda count and the Hare method. As noted in chapter 5, both of those have higher Condorcet efficiency than single-vote, as well. For a variety of reasons, approval voting is the only one of the methods of voting that is a feasible alternative to single-vote.)

Table 6.1 shows that approval voting has higher Condorcet efficiency than single-vote, according to the computer simulations that Merrill ran. Furthermore, it is particularly important to note that single-vote's Condorcet efficiency drops dramatically as the number of candidates proliferates, especially as the number of candidates exceeds three. In fact, this is true with approval voting as well, although approval's Condorcet efficiency easily beats out single-vote in large fields of candidates.

The variation in Condorcet efficiency based on the number of candidates competing has important consequences for presidential nomination campaigns. The violation of the Condorcet criterion is more serious in the critical early states that work to winnow the field of candidates and often provide momentum for successful candidates. In the later states, the field of candidates is usually limited to three, two, or one candidate. The Condorcet violation is either unlikely or impossible in smaller fields of candidates. Even single-vote does well in three-candidate races. It is in the highly influential earlier states that the field of candidates is frequently quite large, making the potential for Condorcet violations greater.

These states usually have the most impact on the race, therefore, the violation of the Condorcet criterion is important because of the probable frequency of violations in the *most important contests in the campaign*. In addition, delegate allocations are then made based on potentially inaccurate reflections of the voters' preferences.

Consistency

Most state parties, whether Democratic or Republican, using either winner-take-all or proportional types of rules, subdivide their states for the purposes of apportioning delegates. Most commonly this subdivision is done by congressional district lines. This sort of practice can violate the consistency fairness principle.

What accounts for this violation even within the framework of the proportional allocation of delegates used by all Democratic states parties and some Republican state parties is the existence of the cut-off percentage for acquiring delegates. The violation of consistency is more serious and more likely to take place with winner-take-all or bonus delegate rules.

Following is the distribution of preferences of all the voters in a hypothetical state primary. This state has thirty voters, as shown below:

	1	2	3	4	5
V(1 - 10)	A	B	C	D	E
V(11 - 21)	B	A	C	D	E
V(22 - 25)	C	B	A	D	E
V(26 - 28)	D	B	A	C	E
V(29 - 30)	E	B	A	C	D

In this state candidate B receives eleven first-place votes to A's ten votes, C's four votes, D's three votes, and E's two votes (using the single-vote method of counting votes). Furthermore, according to the complete preference structure of the voters, B is the Condorcet winner, being preferred in pairwise comparisons to all other candidates.

Now imagine that the state is divided into three congressional districts for the purpose of selecting delegates based on a primary outcome. Ten delegates can be won in each district. A candidate must receive more than 10 percent in a district to receive delegates. After the threshold of 10 percent is taken into consideration, delegates will be allotted on a proportional basis. There are an equal number of voters (ten) in each district.

The voters are divided into their congressional districts as in the following example. Only first-place votes are taken into consideration. Delegates (ten per district) are parceled out proportionally, with candidates required to receive more than 10 percent of the vote to receive delegates.

DISTRICT #1
A - 5 votes
C - 2 votes
B, D, E - 1 vote each
B, D, and E do not qualify for delegates
A receives seven delegates, C receives three delegates, as allotted proportionally among qualifiers.

DISTRICT #2
A - 3 votes
B - 5 votes
C, D - 1 vote each
C and D do not qualify for delegates
B receives six delegates, A receives four, as allotted proportionally among qualifiers.

DISTRICT #3
A - 2 votes
B - 5 votes
C, D, E - one vote each
C, D, and E do not qualify for delegates
B receives seven delegates, A gets three.

The state totals are:
A - 14 delegates
B - 13 delegates
C - 3 delegates

Remember that B received more votes in the state (eleven) than A (ten) and that B is the Condorcet winner in the state, beating all other candidates in pairwise comparisons. But A won more delegates.

This fairness problem, as with the violation of the neutrality criterion, can nearly be alleviated with the elimination of the threshold. If there had been no threshold requirement to qualify for delegates in a district in this state, B would have received more delegates than A, by a count of eleven to ten. There may be, however, practical difficulties with eliminating the threshold. Since states ordinarily allot delegates at the congressional district level, the elimination of the threshold might require the fractionalizing of individual delegate votes.

Independence from Irrelevant Alternatives

As noted in the section on the violation of the neutrality principle, different candidates might survive longer in nomination campaigns depending on which states started out the nomination process. This assertion was made based on the idea that were Tennessee and Arizona to start out the process instead of Iowa and New Hampshire, the voters in those states might choose to give their support to different candidates. Different voters starting the race could have two effects. They might make different candidates viable and serious contenders for the nomination, or they might simply prolong the flight time of different trial-balloon candidacies. Regarding the independence from irrelevant alternatives criterion, the primary concern is the impact of the latter possibility.

In essence, the matter of which candidates stay in the race for how long can potentially have a determinative effect on the outcome of a nomination campaign. It is rather easy to see how "irrelevant alternatives" can have an impact on the current nomination campaign. This simplified model of the nomination campaign that there are just two primaries (held sequentially) to be largely determinative of the outcome of the campaign. The preference orders of the voters in the two states are identical. There are three candidates in the race, at least in the beginning. Imagine that the delegates are allotted with perfect proportionality, with the single-vote method of preference aggregation.

For both states:

	$\underline{1}$	$\underline{2}$	$\underline{3}$
V(1 - 9)	A	B	C
V(10 - 16)	B	A	C
V(17 - 20)	C	B	A

The voting in the first primary would be nine for A, seven for B, and four for C.

If C were to stay in the race for the second primary, the final outcome would be A with eighteen total votes, B with fourteen, and C with eight.

If C were to drop out of the race after the first primary, as is a common effect of the dynamics of these races affecting candidates who finish poorly in early events, A and B would tie with eighteen votes each.

In the first case, A would be in a much more commanding position to woo enough of the delegates C won to get the nomination. In the second case, A and B are in identical positions.

The main point of this hypothetical example is that the timing of withdrawals can have profound effects on the outcomes of serialized elections. A real-world example: John Glenn's efforts to press on into the southern Super Tuesday in 1984 may have cost Gary Hart the opportunity to eliminate Walter Mondale that day. Hart was garnering a great many anti-Mondale votes at this stage of the race. Glenn's continuance in the race diluted the concentration of these votes for Hart.

This violation, as with the violation of undifferentiatedness, is a fairness problem endemic in these serialized elections, although its severity is lessened when the field of candidates is narrowed quickly. When the field of candidates is narrowed quickly, irrelevant trial-balloon alternatives do not have as much opportunity to alter the outcome of subsequent primaries, and potentially the decision as to who will be the nominee.

Discussion

Presidential nomination campaigns can violate all six of Riker's criteria of fairness for electoral arrangements. This would seem, at least on the surface, to be cause for great concern. After all, how can an electoral system that cannot be certain to meet *any* of the standards of fairness be acceptable in a democracy? Not even the most basic tenet of fairness that applies to the electorate—one person-one vote—or its corollary that applies to the candidates—a level playing field—is satisfied by this peculiar electoral process. One would be hard-pressed to invent an electoral system that would have the potential not to meet a single standard of fairness, but this is exactly the result of the evolution of the U.S. presidential nomination process.

This strict social choice analysis of electoral arrangements, however, is only one perspective for assessing a method of public choice. Furthermore, just because an electoral process *can* violate a criterion of fairness does not mean it is likely to. Also, in making an assessment of the presidential nomination process, it is conceivable that the very aspect of the process that violates a criterion of fairness may in other ways improve the quality of the decision-making process.

For these reasons, both the *likelihood* and *severity* of these violations, as well as whether the violations bring with them some advantages to the campaign environment, must be considered. In doing so, a more sophisticated understanding of the public choice problems of the presidential nomination process can be achieved. What follows is a description of the likelihood and severity of the violations, together with an explanation of the reason for the violation.

Undifferentiatedness and Neutrality Violations

The undifferentiatedness violation and the neutrality violation both are inevitable and permanent parts of the nomination process the way it is today, with sequentially scheduled primaries and precinct caucuses. These criteria are important ones for the obvious reason—elections are less democratic if one person-one vote is violated and if the electoral landscape favors some candidates over others. Starting the process of delegate selection in any states would lead to advantages and disadvantages for certain candidates.

As long as delegate selection events are staggered over the course of the primary season and the dynamics of the process remain, as they seem likely to, as described by various scholars and summarized in chapter 3, then these violations are inevitable. These violations are serious ones and occur in every campaign; as a result they merit further attention.

Monotonicity and Independence from Irrelevant Alternative Violations

The monotonicity violation is probably rather unlikely to occur in presidential nomination campaigns. The independence from irrelevant alternatives violation is more likely to occur. These violations occur because of the constantly changing fields of candidates in the nomination races.

Neither of these two violations, however, is severe. The reason is the inexorable, and really ruthless, winnowing of the field of candidates that occurs in presidential nomination campaigns. Trial-balloon candidacies rarely last long in these races, thus the opportunities for violations of these criteria are rather few. Most of the delegates are won in presidential nomination campaigns after the field of candidates is narrowed to only two or three candidates, limiting the potential impact and frequency of these violations.

Condorcet Criterion Violation

This violation is likely to occur, particularly in primaries in which there are more than three candidates competing. The reason for the violation is the existence of multicandidate fields. The severity of the violation is greatest in the early states, in which the field of candidates is almost always the largest.

Since the early states are important in generating momentum for successful candidates and in determining the nature of the field of candidates in later states, the violation of the Condorcet criterion is cause for considerable concern for scholars of public choice questions. Another lesson of the Condorcet violation is that delegate allocation may frequently be based on outcomes that do not reflect accurately the preferences of the voters. For these reasons, this violation merits further consideration and discussion.

Consistency Violation

The consistency violation is rather unlikely on the Democratic side and more likely to occur on the Republican side. The reason for the violation is the use of winner-take-all delegate allocation rules and the use of a threshold for winning delegates with proportional allocation rules. Since the GOP uses winner-take-all in many states, the violations are more likely there. The Republicans might justify the use of winner-take-all rules by the fact that such rules reduce the field of candidates more quickly, allowing the party to rally around a likely nominee earlier in the year, avoiding protracted divisive primary struggles. In any event, violations of this criterion, even with winner-take-all rules, are probably infrequent, and the use of winner-take-all rules is defensible on other grounds.

The Democrats' use of proportional allocation with a threshold makes the violation unlikely and not significant when it does happen.

Table 6.2
Violations of fairness in the contemporary nomination process

Criterion	Reason for Violation
Undifferentiatedness	serialized elections
Neutrality	serialized elections and varying methods of delegate allocation
Monotonicity	changing field of candidates
Condorcet Criterion	multicandidate fields
Consistency	varying methods of delegate allocation
Independence	changing field of candidates

In summary, the violations that are the sources of major concern for scholars of public choice are those of the Condorcet criterion and those of undifferentiatedness and neutrality. All three are either likely to occur in a given campaign (Condorcet criterion violation) or are nearly permanent aspects of the campaigns (undifferentiatedness and neutrality violations). These violations all have the potential to be consequential enough that they may have an impact on the outcome of a given presidential nomination race.

The Effects of Serialization: Public Choice Problems in Presidential Nomination Politics

Serialization Causes Some Problems, Resolves Others

The serialization of events in these nomination campaigns is the reason for the violations of undifferentiatedness and neutrality, as well as the violations of independence from irrelevant alternatives and monotonicity. However, while serialization makes possible the violations of the latter two, the dynamics of the serialized process (that ruthlessly weed out the losing candidates) reduce the likelihood and severity of those violations. In other words, if the dynamics of the process did not reduce the field of candidates, the violations of independence from irrelevant alternatives and monotonicity would be more likely and, especially with independence from irrelevant alternatives, have more potential for impact on the outcomes of these races.

Happily, a process that reduces the field of candidates rather quickly makes the monotonicity and independence from irrelevant alternatives of much less frequency and importance. In other words, the "irrelevant alternatives" have less of an impact on delegate selection and the eventual outcome the earlier in the campaign they are forced out.

The undifferentiatedness and neutrality violations, however, are permanent parts of serialized nomination campaigns. They can only be eliminated with the institution of a national primary. But, as noted in chapter 4, many of the advantages of the current process as a method of public choice—many of the things that enhance the campaign environment—are *because of* the serialization of events.

Serialization is what makes it possible for smaller early states to be influential in the process. This gives less well-heeled candidates a chance to get known and be competitive in later larger states. Also, the serialization of events allows for considerable retail politicking in nomination campaigns, with its salutary effects in comparison to a total reliance on mass media sound-bite campaigning. People can learn about the candidates and the candidates get a feel for the problems of ordinary Americans—virtues both John Kennedy and Jimmy Carter noted while campaigning in small state primaries. Furthermore, serialization may allow candidates in later states the valuable opportunity to reassess the choices (perhaps hastily made) by voters earlier in the campaign. In fact, most of what is *good* about the current process is attributable to serialization.

But the serialized nomination process contains a pair of violations of very basic principles of fairness—in lay terms, one person-one vote and the idea of a level playing field. These must be balanced against some of the advantages offered by serialization that are described above. The only alternative that would correct the fairness violations is the national primary, an event that might present a host of other problems that are addressed in the next chapter. Perhaps the reasonable conclusion to draw at this point is that the benefits of serialization should at least make a person pause before rejecting the current set-up. It is the challenge for the reformer to devise ways to lessen the severity of the violations. This is one of the subjects of chapter 8.

The Condorcet Paradox

As fundamental as any problem with the nomination process from a standpoint of social choice theory is the violation of the Condorcet criterion. Particularly in large fields of candidates, the Condorcet efficiency of single-vote is amazingly weak. Merrill's results indicate that in fields of candidates of five or more, the Condorcet efficiency of single-vote may not even be 50 percent. This is particularly a problem in the small early states in which ordinarily there is a large field of candidates. And, of course, the results in these small early states have a great deal of impact on the campaigns, generating momentum for winners and winnowing out losers. Furthermore, the allocation of delegates is based on the results of primaries that may not actually reflect the preferences of the voters.

In essence, critical determinations in presidential nomination campaigns are probably often made in these early events based on a false premise: that the first-place finisher is truly the most preferred candidate. A problem such as this one surely should give any thinking person pause in endorsing plebiscitary democracy in the sort of arrangements present in U.S. presidential nomination campaigns.

There is, however, a paradox involved here. The winnowing of the field of candidates in these early states works to improve the Condorcet efficiency of the later primaries (to 100 percent, even with single-vote, when the field of candidates is reduced to two). While the potential violation of the Condorcet criterion presents a big problem in the early states, it does not in later primaries, which are usually contested by only two or three candidates.

The paradox is that the weeding out of candidates is done in an environment highly susceptible to violations of the Condorcet criterion, but it is precisely that dynamic that enables primaries in later states not to violate the Condorcet criterion. The trick is to maintain the dynamic that enables later states' primaries to be fair while improving the fairness of the earlier events. This has been, and should continue to be, the central objective of reformers of presidential nomination politics.

Conclusion

This analysis of the presidential nomination process from a strict public choice perspective has yielded some interesting results. For one thing, all of the criteria of fairness can be violated in the current arrangements. Three of the violations merit serious attention because of their likelihood and potential impact on the campaigns. The presidential nomination process invariably violates the principles of undifferentiatedness and neutrality, and it is distressingly likely to violate the Condorcet criterion, especially in the critical early state contests when the field of candidates is large.

There are two crucial lessons to be drawn from social choice theory concerning the presidential nomination process as a method of public choice:

1. Serialization causes two of the three most serious violations of fairness—the violations of undifferentiatedness and neutrality. Yet it is this very serialization of primaries that yields most of the positive qualities associated with the process as a method of public choice. These include the opportunity for voters to learn more about the candidates and candidates to learn more about the voters, the chance that voters in later states can correct hasty judgments made early in the campaign, and the accessibility of the process to candidates with limited resources.

2. The Condorcet paradox points up the fact that improving Condorcet efficiency in many states (later ones after the field of candidates has been reduced) is dependent on the results of the early states in which Condorcet efficiency is distressingly low (before the field of candidates has been reduced).

Should the serialized process be rejected out of hand because of violations of fairness as fundamental as those of undifferentiatedness and neutrality? That might depend on the alternative, and whether an alternative could itself stand up to this level of scrutiny. That is the subject of chapter 7.

We can say some things for certain about the serialized arrangements. Although there may be virtue in keeping them, there does need to be some reform. It is good that the field of candidates is reduced quickly, but the winnowing needs to be done fairly. If possible, something should be done to lessen the excessive influence of certain states starting out the process. And efforts should be made to improve the vote-counting procedures in whatever states start out the process.

Chapter Seven

Assessing the Reform Alternatives

Chapter 6 looked at how fair and democratic the electoral arrangements in the presidential nomination process are. There are some serious problems with these electoral arrangements and the way voters' preferences are aggregated in them. This chapter asks the logical follow-up question: Are the alternatives out there any better?

In chapter 4, three popular comprehensive reform alternatives to the current presidential nomination process were described: the national primary, the convention/national primary, and regional primaries. This chapter makes a thorough assessment and comparison of the these three reform proposals and the current process.

The analysis of the reform alternatives is done using the "Characteristics of a Good Campaign Environment in Presidential Nomination Politics" that was introduced in chapter 4. They are:

1. The electoral arrangements in the process must be fair to the candidates, and votes must be tallied fairly and democratically.

2. Given the commonly large fields of candidates, the public must have a reasonable opportunity to learn about the issue positions, accomplishments, and character of the people running. Candidates, as well, must have a reasonable opportunity to learn the concerns of the public.

3. The process should not permit hastily made judgments to dictate the nomination of a presidential candidate. Because of the high stakes in presidential selection, the public must be given the opportunity to reconsider its initial judgments of the candidates.

4. The process must not have obstacles to entry for candidates that are so burdensome that they discourage the candidacy of potentially good candidates.

First, this chapter addresses characteristic 1—whether the reform alternatives are a fairer form of public choice than the current arrangements by Riker's six criteria of fairness. More specifically it notes whether the alternatives violate as many of the criteria; whether, when there are violations, they are as likely to happen; and whether the violations have the potential to have an impact on the outcome of the campaigns.

It also assesses the reform alternatives by the other three characteristics of a good process of public choice; then engages in some conjecture as to whether the reform alternatives would improve the discourse and decision-making in nomination campaigns.

In the end, regional primaries reform is found to be clearly inferior to the current process. The national primary and the convention/national primary do offer some substantial advantages. The national primary, however, would have a campaign environment potentially not conducive to the informed participation of the public. The convention/national primary may bring with it a fatal flaw as well. In the end, each individual must determine for himself or herself whether either one of these options is preferable to the current process.

Introduction

Several determinations have been made thus far regarding the characteristics of the current process as a method of public choice.

Chapter 6 noted that the current process suffers most from the violations of undifferentiatedness, neutrality, and the Condorcet criterion. In other words, the electoral arrangement is unfair in that it violates the principle of one person-one vote, it systematically favors certain candidates, and the method of tallying votes in the early states carries with it the potential of rewarding undeserving candidates. Although the serialization of primaries causes two of these violations, this same serialization helps to reduce the chance for violations of monotonicity and independence from irrelevant alternatives and can lessen or eliminate the Condorcet criterion violation in later states.

Serialization carries with it numerous other advantages in creating a healthy campaign environment conducive to informed and reflective participation by the public. For example, the current arrangements have been rather open and hospitable to little-known and even poorly funded candidacies. Gary Hart in 1984 and George Bush in 1980 became viable contenders although both were almost unknowns at the start of the race. Hart was not well-funded either, when the race started. Jerry Brown (1992) and Jesse Jackson (1984, 1988), while both relatively well-known, were able to survive and compete throughout the campaign without great financial resources. Nomination politics is remarkably open, with many candidates with large followings receiving a hearing that they never would have in years past.

It should be noted that the continuation of front-loading, described in chapter 3, makes the current arrangements less hospitable to many candidates in 1996 than it was in the races described here, whether the candidates are well-known or not. The start-up costs for a campaign are fast approaching a prohibitive level for many more aspiring candidates than in the recent past.

The importance of the small early states in the current arrangements, especially Iowa and New Hampshire, promotes a good deal of grass-roots retail politicking. This characteristic allows candidates to learn about voters and their concerns and voters to learn about candidates, in ways that are impossible when the focus of the campaign is exclusively advertising and sound-bite-style campaigning. Of course, most of the campaign is conducted through the mass media—but retail politicking does remain an important part of the process as long as there is so much emphasis on small early states. However, this advantage, too, will be lessened as front-loading continues and there are fewer days during the campaign on which only one state holds its primary or precinct caucuses.

There is considerable evidence in recent history that voters do learn a good deal of meaningful information concerning candidates' issue positions, accomplishments, and so on during these campaigns. The problem is that if the nomination is decided quickly (as seems increasingly likely with front-loading), this information cannot be put to use by a large number of voters. It takes a good bit of time for voters to digest and process the information they receive about a half-dozen or so candidates that they knew nothing about a few weeks or months previously.

Judging the Reform Alternatives

Each of the reform alternatives is considered first by the fairness of the electoral arrangements and the method of aggregating voters' preferences. They then are compared with the current arrangements on the basis of the three other key public choice issues listed earlier.

The National Primary

The Fairness Criteria
From the social choice perspective, the institution of a national primary with a run-off stipulation if no candidate receives 40 percent in the first primary is a dramatic improvement over the current arrangements. Here is how the national primary stacks up by Riker's six criteria of fairness.

Undifferentiatedness: No violation of undifferentiatedness would occur with a national primary. All votes would weigh equally on the outcome of the race.

Neutrality: No violation of neutrality would occur with a national primary. The playing field is level when no candidate has the built-in advantage that can occur when the process is serialized and extra emphasis is put on certain of the early states.

Monotonicity: The monotonicity criterion could be violated with the national primary, in a way slightly different from the violation in the current system.

The following example has a field of twenty-one voters, with four candidates. The preference structure of the public is as follows (dashes indicate irrelevant preference):

	1	2	3	4
V(1-5)	W	X	-	-
V(6-11)	X	-	-	-
V(12-13)	Y	X	-	-
V(14-17)	Y	W	-	-
V(18-21)	Z	W	X	Y

In this scenario, Y and X would make the runoff with six votes each. The runoff would be won by X since the other 9 voters prefer X to Y.

But what if voters 12 and 13 raised their evaluation of X ahead of Y? This would take Y out of the runoff. X would have eight votes, W would have five, and Y would receive only four. A runoff between X and W is won by W, since voters 14-21 prefer W to X. Thus, X's improved showing in the first primary, based on the support by voters 12 and 13 actually cost him the nomination! This is a violation of monotonicity.

This violation, as with the violation of monotonicity in the current arrangement, is not likely to happen. It is no more cause for concern than the violation as it applies in the current arrangements.

Condorcet Criterion: The violation of the Condorcet criterion is far less likely to occur in a national primary with a runoff than in the current arrangement. For the Condorcet winner to be eliminated, he or she would have to fail to be in one of the top *two* positions in the first primary. The Condorcet efficiency of runoffs, even with single-vote, is much higher than if there is no run-off stipulation.

Consistency: The consistency violation is eliminated with the use of a national primary. There are no subdivisions of the electorate with the national primary; the subdividing of the electorate for the purpose of delegate allocation is the cause of this violation in the current process.

Independence from Irrelevant Alternatives: The violation of independence from irrelevant alternatives is eliminated with the national primary. This violation in the current process is a consequence of the changing field of candidates during the campaign, something that does not happen with the national primary.

In sum, most of the public choice problems with the current nomination process are either eliminated (undifferentiatedness, neutrality, consistency, independence from irrelevant alternatives) or mitigated (Condorcet criterion) by the national primary. The only similar violation is that of monotonicity, a violation unlikely to occur with either method. Employing the analytical tools of social choice theory yields an unequivocal result when comparing the national primary with the current serialized process of delegate selection: the national primary is a great improvement over an unreformed presidential nomination process.

The National Primary Campaign Environment

Obviously the national primary would change the environment in presidential nomination campaigns radically. Several aspects might be different.

The nomination process likely would be much less open and might tend to discourage people from running for president. The financial burden of competing nationally, even were generous matching funds to be offered, would be tremendous. The burden might constitute an insuperable obstacle for almost anyone. Only those with established national reputations and, more important, fund-raising networks could hope to compete. Surely many would be discouraged on those grounds alone. If the financial burden of running in the current process discourages potentially good presidents from running, the situation only would be made worse with a national primary.

The national primary would, of course, eliminate the early testing grounds in small states. This would remove much of the opportunity voters have in some states to see the candidates at the grass-roots level. Retail politicking, so prominent in some states in the current process, would be reduced markedly in a national primary. Candidates, to win nationally, would have to focus on areas with large populations, probably to the exclusion of most smaller states. As such, there would be less of an opportunity for candidates to learn about the voters. The focus on small states in the current process has the effect of *forcing* candidates to meet people and learn about them at the local level; this sort of contact might be avoided by candidates in a national event.

As a result of the relative absence of grass-roots politicking in the national primary because of the need to focus campaign efforts nationally, there would be an increase in the emphasis on mass media politics. It would be necessary for all candidates to conduct national media campaigns to be competitive. While grass-roots organization and vote mobilization still would be components of campaigns, they would be less important than in the current process relative to the need to reach the mass public through advertising and free media.

It is difficult to say whether voters would learn more about the candidates in the national primary than in the current process. Certainly the learning process that the public would experience would be very different. In the current process there is evidence that voters learn a good deal about the contenders if they are given the time to process information.

No such similar opportunity would be afforded in a one-shot deal such as the national primary. So on the one hand, voters may not have as much time to process information. But on the other hand, there surely would be a more intense focus on the candidates in the national media, and debates and forums (that would surely be a part of national primaries) might attract high levels of attention from the public—although large multicandidate forums tend to degenerate quickly into chaotic battles to put forth the pithiest sound bite for the evening news.

The likely result of this sort of environment is that voters would not cope well if the field of candidates exceeded three in the national primary. Voters might more reasonably be expected to place and evaluate candidates when the field was small.

There certainly would not be the time for sober reevaluation of and reflection on hastily made judgments as there potentially is over the course of a longer primary season.

Convention/National Primary

The Fairness Criteria
The convention that chooses the candidates for the national primary in this reform cannot be judged by the public choice criteria, since it is not a method of public choice. Instead, in considering the criteria of fairness, the national primary that would follow the convention that would be contested by two or three candidates is evaluated. The convention is considered in relation to the other characteristics of a good campaign environment. In the main, the national primary in this format is a dramatic improvement over the current process by the public choice criteria. To summarize:

Undifferentiatedness: The potential for an undifferentiatedness violation is eliminated. All voters are treated equally in the national primary held after the convention.

Neutrality: The potential for a neutrality violation is eliminated as well. A national primary provides a level playing field as an electoral arrangement.

Monotonicity: The potential for a monotonicity violation is eliminated. Unlike the first national primary reform, this reform has no run-off stipulation, making the monotonicity violation impossible.

Condorcet Criterion: There is the possibility to violate this criterion. In the case in which three candidates qualify for the primary, single-vote does have a significant potential to identify someone other than the Condorcet winner. Still, single-vote has a pretty high Condorcet efficiency with three candidates, and, of course, 100 percent Condorcet efficiency with two. Presumably many times the convention would select only two candidates for the national primary. Thus, the problem of the Condorcet criterion violation is much less severe with the convention/national primary reform than with the current process.

Consistency: The potential for a consistency violation is eliminated. Consistency violations can occur when the electorate is subdivided; this does not happen with a national primary.

Independence from Irrelevant Alternatives: The potential for a violation of independence from irrelevant alternatives is eliminated. The field of candidates does not change with a one-shot national primary.

From a purely public choice standpoint, this reform resolves or substantially lessens the violations of all the criteria of fairness in comparison with the current arrangements. The only remaining violation is the Condorcet criterion violation, but even this one is made much less likely since the field of candidates is limited to three.

The Convention/National Primary Campaign Environment

The convention/national primary reform alternative would change the landscape of nomination politics dramatically, in many of the same ways that the national primary would. But there would be some important differences from the pure national primary.

Perhaps the critical distinction would be that, in some years, the convention/national primary would remove the participatory element in nomination politics—that is, there would not be a campaign environment. If the convention, constituted of the state central committees, could settle on a nominee with a special majority of two-thirds, or if a candidate received greater than 50 percent of the votes with no competitor receiving more than 25 percent, then there would be no primary. This eventuality would constitute a radical change in presidential nomination politics. It would reinstitute the possibility of a party-dominated system.

The purpose of this reform is to revive the influence of the organizational party in presidential nomination politics. The process is, in effect, intentionally arranged to be more closed. Of course, in almost every state the state parties choose their leadership at the grass-roots level in democratic ways. But the selection of candidates at the convention to compete in the national primary (were there to be one) would be a step removed from the selection of the party leadership. In an important sense, then, the process would not be open to anyone wishing to run under the party banner.

A process such as the convention/national primary would make it next to impossible that a candidate with little notoriety could make it to the national primary. Receiving greater than a quarter of the support of party officials around the country would be no mean feat. It probably could be achieved only by a candidate who already was well-known or well-financed enough to make connections with party leaders around the country. The experience of John Kennedy in the years leading up to his nomination in 1960 comes to mind. Although not as well-known as some of his competitors, he had the resources to court successfully important figures in the party around the country. Little-known candidates would be far less likely to be successful, or even be viable contenders, with this reform.

Of course, with the convention/national primary, there would be no early testing grounds in small primary or precinct caucus states as with today's process. Public retail politicking would not play a large part in a process such as this one. There would be considerable politicking at the state and local levels to win the votes of party officials at the convention, but it likely would take place within party meetings, and not so much in public events.

In the primary, with this reform (if there is a primary), there would necessarily be an increase in emphasis on the mass media. A national event pitting two or three candidates against each other in a primary would be contested largely through the media, whether in paid advertising or free coverage (debates, speeches, and so on). The focus in a national primary would be on the states and regions with greater concentrations of people, making much of the retail politicking that currently goes on unnecessary for the candidates to conduct. The nomination process would be much less of a learning process than it is in the intensely public process that exists today. As with the national primary, candidates could avoid meeting voters at the retail level and avoid having the opportunity thrust on them to learn about the voters.

It is an open question whether voters would learn much about the candidates in a national primary, as it has been shown they do given time in the current process. But the issue of voters learning about candidates is a more complex one with this reform. Keep in mind that one of the purposes of having the convention determine the candidates is to take some of the burden of judging the quality of the candidates off the voters, a burden that advocates of this reform say is properly borne to a far greater extent than is currently the case by party insiders.

It is true that the voters might have to make the final decision, and, as such, what they learn about the candidates is very important. But in a critical sense this reform leaves much of the responsibility for picking acceptable candidates to the party elite, leaving the public only to pick from among a short list of acceptable candidates. Certainly in the national primary, with only two or three candidates competing, voters have at least an opportunity to learn about the candidates.

Regional Primaries

The Fairness Criteria
Unlike the national primary reforms, the regional primaries reform is a mixed bag from the standpoint of the strict public choice criteria. Looking at the reform from this perspective, in some respects it improves on the current arrangements; in other ways it it is worse.

Undifferentiatedness: Undifferentiatedness still would be violated with regional primaries. Some voters would be very likely to have more influence on the outcome of the race than others. In most cases, the participants in the first two regional events would have far more impact than those in the last three events. One could say that the violation is a little less severe with regional primaries than with the current arrangement because more voters would be included in the event that would make the critical determination as to which candidate or candidates would survive. In the current setup, many of the candidates are weeded out after the participation of voters in only two or three states. If the first regional event were to play a similar role, at least the voters in ten states would have a say about the viability of the candidates.

Neutrality: Neutrality still would be violated with regional primaries, and in much the same manner as in the current arrangements. Some candidates are better positioned than others in certain regions. The potential for a candidate to survive the first regional event could rest on his strength in that region. This is, of course, a direct violation of neutrality in much the same manner it is violated in the current process, as was discussed in chapter 6.

Monotonicity: Monotonicity, too, could be violated in the regional primaries reform. The violation could occur in much the same way, as illustrated in chapter 6, as it does in the current process.

Condorcet Criterion: The Condorcet criterion also could be violated with regional primaries. The violation could have an even more profound impact with regional primaries than with the current arrangements.

The main issue with the Condorcet violation in the current process is that critical determinations are made in large fields of candidates in the small early states. The existence of large fields of candidates is what is problematical here, because Condorcet efficiency is lowest in those circumstances. In the current process the critical determinations are made in states with few delegates. In the first regional event, a candidate who is not the Condorcet winner might, in a large multicandidate field, do well across a broad region and win hundreds of delegates.

In the current setup, were there to be misleading early results, at least only a few delegates would be allocated on the basis of the results. Misleading results are a serious issue when momentum is at stake, as is the case in today's process, even if there are only a few delegates being contested. The problem is yet more serious when momentum *and* large numbers of delegates are at stake, as would be the case with regional primaries.

Consistency: Consistency could be violated with regional primaries in much the same way as in the current process, since delegates still would be allocated according to state rules, and states usually divide by congressional districts in allocating delegates.

Independence from Irrelevant Alternatives: Independence from irrelevant alternatives could be violated in much the same way as in the current process, as the field of candidates would change with regional primaries, as it does in the current process.

The existence of sequential delegate selection events and the potential for changing fields of candidates with regional primaries make the reform very similar from a strictly social choice standpoint to the current process. Both can violate all six criteria. Regional primaries mitigate slightly the undifferentiatedness violation by allowing more voters in on the crucial early winnowing of the field of candidates. However, the potential for a Condorcet criterion violation has more serious implications with regional primaries than with the current arrangements.

The Regional Primaries Campaign Environment

Regional primaries would produce a campaign environment that would look much like the current process—but maybe be a bit worse. Essentially, most of the characteristics of the current process would be exaggerated, usually for the worse.

Regional primaries would be very likely to present barriers to more potential candidates than exist in the current arrangements. The start-up costs for presidential campaigns are considerable in today's system, especially with the continual front-loading that is taking place. But the prospect of facing a ten-state primary to start out a campaign is a far more daunting obstacle to a prospective candidate than the current situation in which Iowa and New Hampshire lead off the first few weeks of the campaign season. It simply would be far more difficult for a candidate to become viable in a region than in a couple of small states.

Regional primaries would of course remove the predominance of small early states such as New Hampshire and Iowa. The first test would be in an entire region instead. Regional primaries, as demonstrated by the ad hoc creation of a southern primary, are characterized less by town meetings and retail politicking than by a tarmac-to-tarmac style of campaigning. Most candidates in the southern Super Tuesdays have found it extremely hard to make their presence felt in more than a few states. Of course, there would be more time to get established in the first region than there has been in these Super Tuesday extravaganzas, but advertising in more than a few of the states would not be feasible for most of the candidates. In essence, the advantages that come with the small early tests would be lost with this reform.

As a result, regional primaries would have a substantial emphasis on mass media campaigning. With the absence of the focus on a group of small early primary states, there would be an increase in the emphasis on mass media campaigning at the expense of retail politicking.

It should be noted that, since the regional primaries are not a one-day affair and are spread over a few months, voters would have the opportunity to learn about the candidates, much as is the case in the current arrangements. The learning process described in chapter 3 is characterized by voters being better able to perceive candidates' ideological positions and career accomplishments, and being in a better position to make judgments about candidates' character, over the course of several weeks. For the candidates surviving the early cut in the first regional event, the opportunity for this sort of learning process for the voters probably would continue with this reform.

There is, however, a big qualification to this advantage. The high costs of regional events might work to eliminate weaker candidates before voters would have the opportunity for reconsideration. This is the danger of having as many as ten states—some of which would be heavily populated with lots of delegates at stake—start the delegate selection season. If the first event were fairly decisive in one candidate's favor, there might not be any opportunity for sober reflection. In other words, while voters might well learn a good deal, the nomination might be a fait accompli by the time the information was processed.

Would candidates learn of the voters' concerns with regional primaries? They probably would learn less than with the current arrangements (again, the difference is not great with front-loading) but more than with the national primary. Regional primaries would force candidates into a long and grueling campaign season, a campaign in which successful candidates might have to compete in every part of the country. While the opportunity for one-to-one and small group contact with voters would be less than with the current process because of the absence of one-state primary days in small and accessible states, the candidates would have to travel and invariably, learn a great deal in the process of competing in and surviving five regional events.

Comparing and Contrasting

The Fairness Criteria

The following is a summary of the three reform alternatives as they compare to the current process by Riker's six criteria of fairness.

Undifferentiatedness: Both the national primary and the convention/national primary reform eliminate the possibility of the undifferentiatedness violation. Every person's vote carries the same weight in a national event. With regional primaries, it is likely that the voters in the first and second regions will be particularly influential in determining, the field of viable contenders and perhaps the winner if most candidates drop out early.

Neutrality: Again, both of the reforms that have national primaries remove the possibility of the neutrality violation. No candidate would have an unfair advantage by virtue of the electoral arrangements in a national event. The regional primaries reform surely would favor some candidates who might perform better in the region where the first primaries were held.

Monotonicity: Only the convention/national primary reform removes the potential for this violation. A changing field of candidates over time (whether in a runoff or in serialized primaries) creates the possibility for this violation. The convention/ national primary has no run-off stipulation.

Condorcet Criterion: While none of the reforms alleviate the chance for a violation of this criterion, the national primary and convention/national primary lessen the chance considerably. Regional primaries may work to exacerbate the problem associated with the Condorcet violation by having more delegates chosen in an event that may have a multicandidate field.

Consistency: The consistency criterion cannot be violated with either reform that has a national primary. Consistency can be violated with regional primaries.

Independence from Irrelevant Alternatives: Independence from irrelevant alternatives cannot be violated with either reform that has a national primary. Regional primaries can violate the criterion in much the same manner as the current process can.

Table 7.1
Rankings by the criteria of social choice

First   Convention/National Primary
violates only the Condorcet criterion, but is not likely to do so

Second   National Primary
violates only the Condorcet criterion (but not likely with run-off stipulation) and monotonicity

Third   Current Process
violates all six criteria

Fourth   Regional Primaries
violates all six criteria—mitigates undifferentiatedness and neutrality slightly compared to the current process, but exacerbates the Condorcet criterion since far more delegates are chosen than in the current arrangements when the field of candidates is likely to be large

---

It is very clear that, by the criteria of social choice theory, both the national primary and the convention/national primary are far superior to the current arrangements or regional primaries. The national primary reform shares only the monotonicity and Condorcet criterion violations with the current arrangement. While the Condorcet criterion merits very serious attention, the stipulation for a runoff following the national primary has the advantage of lessening the risk of violating that criterion. The convention/national primary reform does not violate monotonicity, and it similarly lessens the likelihood of the Condorcet criterion violation.

Regional primaries share most of the characteristics of the current arrangement when viewed from this perspective. This is because both the reform and the existing system are characterized by serialized events and changing fields of candidates, two qualities that present most of the difficulties from the social choice perspective. The most serious of the violations, that of the Condorcet criterion, is actually made worse with regional primaries, since more rides on the first event (in terms of delegates) when the field of candidates might be large and the Condorcet efficiency is dangerously low.

On the public choice criteria, the rankings are clear (see table 7.1). The best process is the convention/national primary, with only a significantly reduced violation of the Condorcet criterion. It is followed closely by the national primary, which has a significantly reduced Condorcet violation, as well as the minor violation of the monotonicity principle.

In the second tier are the current process and regional primaries. Both violate all six criteria. The current process is slightly superior to the regional primaries because the regional primaries' violation of the Condorcet criterion is particularly problematical.

The Campaign Environment

The *current process* is characterized by an openness even to candidates with fairly modest resources, crucial testing grounds in small states where grass-roots organizational and retail politics are at a premium, some opportunity for voters to learn about the candidates' ideology and character, and an extended and constant campaigning period that forces candidates to learn a great deal about the voters and their concerns.

Some of these characteristics of the process gradually are being diluted and modified by the front-loading of the primaries. Front-loading has the effect of reducing the openness of the process to lesser-known potential candidates, because of the imminence of primaries in big states such as New York and California. It probably will have the effect of increasing the emphasis on mass media campaigns, concomitantly reducing the emphasis on grass-roots politics. Also, voters will have less of an opportunity to learn about the candidates and to reconsider hastily made judgments as the races are likely to be decided more quickly.

The *national primary* shares some of the qualities of the current process, although it tends to amplify them. It would be, for example, the ultimate ratification of direct participatory democracy in presidential nomination politics. The national primary would be even more influenced by mass media campaigning.

On the other hand, the national primary would differ in some ways. It would be much less open to the large number of candidates who entertain serious notions about running for president in today's environment. This is because the financial hurdles would be even greater. There would be no small state testing grounds, and consequently much less retail and grass-roots politicking. Thus, the candidates would have less of an opportunity for sustained contact with the people. Although it is an open question, it is entirely possible that voters would not have the same opportunity to learn about the candidates as they do today. If voters were confronted with a list of six or eight candidates, it might not be reasonable for them to be able to digest information about them; however, were only two or three candidates to run, the attention given them might make it possible for voters to learn their issue positions and other information relevant to an informed judgment. It is certain that voters would not have the opportunity to reconsider decisions made by early state voters as can happen with the current process.

The *convention/national primary* reform would, when a primary is held, also offer a heavy dose of direct democracy. There would be considerable mass media campaigning during such a national primary.

There would, however, be many changes in the campaign environment with this reform. Candidates would have to appeal to insiders to get convention votes, making the process far less open to candidates than it is today. There would, of course, be no early testing grounds and the consequent preponderance of retail politicking. Candidates would learn less about the voters, and voters might learn less about the candidates. (But advocates of the reform emphasize that this is the advantage of the reform—it does not expect voters to do well what they cannot, that is, sift through information about a large number of candidates.) Most important, the parties would reestablish a considerable degree of control in the process, leaving the process far less open to insurgency within the parties.

Regional primaries offer many of the qualities of the current process. Mass media politicking would be perhaps even more commonplace. Voters, with the extended campaign, would have the time and opportunity to learn a great deal about the candidates. Candidates, as well, would be forced into every region of the country and would have the opportunity to learn a great deal. However, this knowledge might prove irrelevant if only one candidate emerged from the first primary.

The only major difference between regional primaries and the current process is in the area of the small state testing grounds. The regional primaries reform does not have this characteristic. As a result there would be less grass-roots and retail politicking than occurs currently.

Conclusion

What can be said for certain in comparing the reform alternatives with the current process? Perhaps the only "certainty" is that there is no clear choice.

From the strict public choice perspective, the national primary offers a considerably fairer electoral arrangement. But this is at the cost of eliminating much of the grass-roots campaigning and the openness to modestly financed candidates that exists currently.

The convention/national primary solves almost all the problems of technical electoral fairness, but also at the expense of grass-roots politics. Its most noticeable characteristic is that such a reform is an attempt in part to close off the parties' nomination processes from insurgency. In effect, this process limits the field of candidates that the voters have to pick from. But this is entirely intentional, since one of the main aims of reviving the party role is so that insiders can pass judgment on the fitness of potential presidential candidates. This quality of the process makes it the most radical proposal for change. Much more is said about the dangers and the advantages of this reform in chapter 8.

The regional primaries reform offers little improvement in terms of technical fairness, except that the elimination of the emphasis on New Hampshire and Iowa mitigates slightly the undifferentiatedness and neutrality violations. (Still, this is more than balanced out by the tendency of the regional primaries to exacerbate the Condorcet problem by making more ride on the outcome of the first regional event when the field of candidates is likely to be large.)

Regional primaries do offer the advantage of the opportunity for learning on the part of the candidates and the voters in a participatory environment, in a way perhaps approximating the current process. It probably would not be as open to as many candidates since the financial hurdle of competing in a region would be greater than that posed by Iowa and New Hampshire.

So is radical reform necessary to correct the weaknesses of the current process? The answer to this question is a judgment call. At this point, it is clear that regional primaries as commonly proposed offer the prospect of little if any improvement over the current process and the possibility of substantially harming the campaign environment by creating more obstacles for candidates and reducing the chance voters have to reconsider hastily made judgments. It also makes the Condorcet violation more serious.

However, the national primary and the convention/national primary do offer some substantial improvements. The national primary reforms are far better by the fairness criteria, and the convention/national primary offers the bonus (some feel) of reviving the organizational party in presidential nomination politics.

But these improvements come with costs attached: with a national primary, the campaign would be totally dominated by mass media politics; with the convention/national primary, there might also be that sort of politics, but the more important consequence would be the closing off of the nomination process in the two major parties to insurgent movements. What should be done? The answer to that question is the main subject of the chapter 8.

Chapter Eight

Summary and Conclusions

The presidential nomination process has evolved, with minimal planning, into the type of open, participatory, and essentially plebiscitary campaign that it is today. It is a part of and a reflection of the developments in recent decades in the U.S. political process and within the political parties at all levels and branches of government.

This book shows, over the course of the history of the parties, the process for nominating presidential candidates became increasingly candidate centered, with more and more influence wielded by the participating public. The representative party-elite-centered legitimation of presidential nominees gradually gave way to the plebiscitary legitimation that has characterized the process for about the past twenty-five years. At all levels and branches of U.S. politics, not the least of which within the political parties, procedural changes and reform usually have been in the direction of more direct participation by the public.

At all levels of U.S. politics, candidates for office are not anointed by an elite. In the term popularized by journalist Alan Ehrenhalt, candidates today are *self-nominated.* This is certainly true of presidential candidates. It is only in the very loosest sense of the term party that one can say that the parties nominate presidential candidates. Candidates put themselves forward, and the people who choose to participate, or who are convinced to participate, vote to nominate one of the candidates to run as the standard-bearer of a party. Running for office at all levels is like starting a business. Raising money is the first priority, and along with that comes the creation of a large organization replete with specialists in polling, strategy, advertising, and fund-raising. Most of this effort is undertaken independent of the organizational parties.

The delegate selection phase of the presidential nomination campaign is made up of a series of about thirty-five primaries and fifteen open precinct caucuses held over a three-and-a-half-month period. But the most grueling part of the presidential campaign is the year or years prior to the first delegate selection event during which time preparations for the campaign are made. This "Invisible

Primary" is an ordeal for the candidate consisting of fund-raiser after fund-raiser and nonstop efforts to line up support across the country. Only the most committed, ambitious, and driven can withstand the withering pace of constant campaigning and fund-raising over a period of months and years. Ultimately candidates must compete for voter support in the primaries and caucuses to win enough delegates to get the party's nomination at the summer national convention.

The increasingly public nature of these campaigns was never really planned by either of the parties. Presidential nomination politics began notably to be characterized by the vigorous activity and campaigning of candidate-centered organizations by the 1950s, but much of the politicking still remained within party meetings around the country until the 1970s. Over the entire course of the century, these party meetings where delegates were selected were becoming gradually more open to insurgency by candidates running, for all intents and purposes, independent campaigns uncontrolled by party officials.

On the Republican side, the great breakthrough for an insurgent campaign came when Barry Goldwater secured the nomination in 1964. He did so largely because of his campaign's success in infiltrating and controlling the delegate selection machinery in the nascent Republican party organizations in the states of the Old Confederacy.

The Democrats officially made all of their party meetings that led to delegate selection open for the 1972 campaign. Precinct caucuses and subsequent party meetings that year came to be controlled by the energetic supporters of insurgent-turned-insider George McGovern. (After all, he was one of the ones to *write* the new rules that magically made insurgents potential insiders.) He rode his strength in these newly opened party meetings to a nomination victory. Both the McGovern and Goldwater insurgencies resulted in landslide defeats of historical proportions for their respective parties in the November general election.

Really beginning in 1972, but even more so in the campaigns after that, there was a sudden upsurge in the number of presidential primaries for both parties. Both parties held publicly contested, primary-dominated nomination campaigns in 1976, contested by about a dozen candidates on the Democratic side and by President Gerald Ford and Ronald Reagan on the Republican side. By 1976 many party leaders, particularly on the Democratic side, had chosen to institute these primaries to select delegates instead of using the newly open party caucuses that had led to the disastrous candidacy of George McGovern. The Republicans chose not to buck the trend that was developing at that time in favor of greater public participation and direct democracy in presidential nomination campaigns.

Every nomination race since 1972 has been a plebiscitary campaign, dominated by public campaigning, in which nearly all the delegates are chosen based on the results of some form of direct democracy, whether in open precinct caucuses and other party meetings or, most commonly, in primaries.

To put this development in historical perspective, presidential nomination politics was rather late in coming to direct democracy. Nomination politics at all other levels of public office in most of the country had long been characterized by plebiscitary forms of democracy. The major parties have either explicitly (in the case of the Democrats) or implicitly (in the case of the Republicans) endorsed participatory forms of democracy and the plebiscitary legitimation for about twenty years now in presidential nomination politics. In this mass media age of instant and direct forms of public participation and avenues for expressing opinions, there is every reason to think that this sort of democracy in presidential nomination politics is here to stay. Presidential nomination politics has become a method of public choice.

This peculiar form of public choice is fraught with difficulties from the standpoint of technical democratic fairness. It is not like most forms of electoral politics in this country, which usually only carry the potential to violate one of the standards of fairness.

Most general elections are contested by only two candidates, a Democrat and a Republican. A two-candidate electoral procedure violates no standards of fairness from the perspective of social choice theory. Any primary contested by more than two candidates, which is fairly common in the United States, may violate one of the standards, the Condorcet criterion. The odd setup of the presidential nomination campaign, with serialized elections and changing fields of candidates, can lead to violations of all standards of fairness.

The way presidential candidates are nominated is not a planned or well thought out process. It has developed in ad hoc fashion, with little consideration of the issues of public choice raised in this book. The process receives criticism on several grounds: the unfairness of the method of aggregating votes, the tilted playing field with the same states year after year having disproportionate impact on the outcome, the decreasing ability of the public to learn and weigh important information about the candidates (and the candidates to learn the concerns of the voters), the decreasing capacity of the public to make informed and even reflective choices in the environment that exists, and the contention that the rigors of the campaign discourage better-qualified candidates.

What can be done about this much maligned process for selecting the candidates for president of the United States? The stakes are huge, of course, since the president plays such an important role in domestic policy and an even more crucial role as a relatively unobstructed player on the stage of international politics, able to order the most powerful military force in the world to exercise its might essentially at his whim. There is a surfeit of ideas to improve the process of selection. The aim of this book is to develop a means to assess these ideas and ultimately to offer some original proposals for reform.

In the remaining pages it first is argued that the comprehensive ideas for restructuring nomination politics discussed in chapters 4 through 7 are either fatally flawed or unrealistic and should not be considered seriously as alternatives to the current arrangements. But the presidential nomination process today is itself flawed and getting worse. In view of that, an original three-part reform proposal is offered that targets the main shortcomings of today's process.

Is Radical Reform Necessary?

The shortcomings of the current nomination process have prompted calls for reform ever since the process became dominantly plebiscitary in the 1970s. Most of the calls for reform have recognized the inevitability of direct democracy in presidential nomination politics. The reforms discussed in this book are among the most commonly proposed comprehensive alternatives that stress direct democratic procedures.

Two of the three reforms (national primary and convention/national primary) would constitute dramatic improvements on the basis of the social choice criteria of fairness. The regional primaries reform, perhaps the most popular reform idea, does not. The next section takes a critical look at these reforms, making the case that none of them is a viable alternative to the current arrangements.

Regional Primaries

The main aim of the reformers supporting regional primaries over the years is to remedy the media overemphasis and disproportionate impact in the current process of small states with unrepresentative populations. Certainly the regional primaries reform does address this problem, replacing the critical first tests in Iowa and New Hampshire with an entire region that would be more diverse than these two states.

But regional primaries offer no improvement over the current arrangements. The campaign environment is worse, offering voters less of an opportunity to reconsider hastily made judgments, perhaps less of a chance to learn about candidates, and presenting candidates with greater obstacles to entry into the contest. The Condorcet criterion violation also is made worse with regional primaries, making this reform no improvement in terms of fairness.

The concept of regional primaries should be rejected. Even its main advantage—reducing the bias of unrepresentative small states—can be addressed without having to accept the weaknesses of this reform.

Convention/National Primary

The convention/national primary deals very successfully with the public choice weaknesses of the current process. It eliminates five of the six violations, and it reduces very substantially the possibility of a Condorcet criterion violation.

No reform for presidential nomination politics is more radical than this one. It combines a national plebiscite with revivified and powerful national conventions for the parties. This gives it both a pure form of direct democracy at the same time as it reinjects the institutional party into the process.

The powerful convention essentially requires the parties' elites to pass on the candidates before they make it to the public phase of the campaign in the national primary. The advantage is that the convention reinstitutes an insiders' peer review of the candidates. Candidates, in being forced to make connections in the party to reach the primary, presumably also would participate in tieing themselves more closely to the parties' institutional framework on a permanent basis. If the institutional party can really help presidents govern in this day and age, the fruits of that might be realized with the enactment of this reform.

The national primary itself would be a massive media event, with the qualifying candidates forced to conduct a national campaign focusing on the most densely populated parts of the country. There are, of course, drawbacks to this sort of event, particularly in its absence of retail politicking, its tremendous cost, and the reduced opportunity for voters to reconsider hastily made judgments.

Of course, advocates of this reform would counter that the convention phase of the campaign would be characterized by candidates traveling the country wooing party insiders in ways that would build the parties' strength at the grass roots. Perhaps the paramount advantage of this reform is that the parties would only pass on to the voters a short list of candidates who might be broadly acceptable to the rank and file in terms of ideology and who would pass whatever character test that the elites cared to administer, thus making it unnecessary for voters to make distinctions that they are not equipped to make in large fields of candidates.

To many, this reform almost sounds perfect. It preserves a critical and potentially decisive role for the public as it attempts to shore up the weaknesses of the most important intermediary institution in any functioning democracy.

Its weakest point is probably that it would effectively close off the process to many aspiring candidates who get a reasonably fair public hearing in the current arrangements. This reform is a radical change in that it makes the party insiders the ones to pass judgment on the candidates at the initial phase of the campaign instead of the public. While five to ten candidates often show their wares in Iowa and New Hampshire, hoping to survive to later, bigger states, in this reform the insiders would do the winnowing at the convention, leaving the public to decide among the top two or three candidates. And when the party insiders developed a consensus of sorts at the convention, no role at all would be left for the public in determining the nominee.

This rejuvenation of the parties' role runs counter to all the historical trends pointing in the direction of a greater role for the public in an increasingly direct and participatory nomination process. Perhaps most important, in a country with a long-standing tradition of only two major parties, limiting choices offered to the public, as this reform does, would be likely to attract powerful, and maybe overwhelming, public opposition.

The two parties *chose* to open up their procedures. This choice was, more than anything else, a necessary adjustment to the social and political climate. The parties risked falling out of favor—it may be the case that the continuation of the dominance of the Democratic and Republican parties in our politics depended on their opening up their procedures to the public over the course of the century. In a tremendously diverse country, regionally, ethnically, and economically, two closed and elite-controlled parties could not conceivably have hoped to maintain their dominance. The adjustments in the direction of openness were rational responses by these institutions to diverse and constantly changing constituencies.

It might be argued that the parties *are* rapidly falling out of favor. It is important to note, however, that had the parties *not* opened up, they most certainly would have met their demise by now in U.S. politics.

In today's politics, it could be said that both of the parties have become so open that the concept of closing out even most fringe groups has become unthinkable. Quite frankly, the ethos of participation is so strong within the parties that this reform is never likely to see the light of day.

In conclusion, this reform is at the same time so radical and reactionary, so counter to historical trends, that its imposition must be deemed extremely unlikely, barring a fundamental change in the U.S. party system. Democrats or Republicans choosing to close up their process in this way is really not a realistic possibility—and might lead directly to their demise.

But what if there were a fundamental restructuring of the party system, perhaps with the election of an independent president? Certainly, in the event this happened, the existing parties, and any new ones, would be looking for different ways to nominate candidates as a response to a profoundly changed political landscape. The convention/national primary alternative has advantages over the national primary, as well as regional primaries, and might then deserve serious consideration.

National Primary

The case for a national primary, although not made as often as it once was, is harder to reject on the grounds that the convention/national primary can be rejected. It most certainly does not run counter to the historical trends of U.S. political parties. Actually, it could be viewed as the logical completion of the gradual opening of the parties this century. It effectively eliminates the "middle man"—the convention delegates who have evolved to be *delegates* in the true sense of the word, carrying out the wishes of voters in their home states with no opportunity for deliberation or independent judgment. The national primary would make permanent and official the plebiscitary character of the process, possibly even to the extent of eliminating the charade known as the national convention.

In terms of the criteria of social choice, the national primary neatly resolves or reduces considerably the most important of the public choice difficulties of the current process. Undifferentiatedness and neutrality are eliminated, and the Condorcet violation is made much less severe with the run-off stipulation. From a strictly social choice perspective, therefore, there is no doubt that the national primary is a vast improvement. But what would a national primary campaign look like?

To compete nationally, in hopes of making a runoff, prospective candidates would have to raise huge amounts of money to get their names known to a sufficient number of people. Candidates would need to raise, independent of federal matching money, at least ten million dollars, and maybe as much as fifteen or twenty million dollars, to be viable. This situation would needlessly discourage good presidential prospects. Presumably the parties would host forums so the candidates could reach a broad audience at no cost, but it is debatable whether these forums would be watched by a large number of people.

Such a campaign would be waged almost entirely through television ads, and the focus of the candidates would necessarily be the parts of the country where the largest number of votes are: California, the big cities in the northeast and middle west, Texas, and Florida. The opportunity for the candidates to get a feel for the country, and the country for the candidates, would be lost, as retail politicking would become a waste of resources and time for the candidates.

It is a judgment call whether a process with these characteristics is better than the current one. At this writing in January 1996, some pundits claim that the GOP race for the nomination is shaping up to look much like what is described in the previous paragraph. For example, the major candidates—Senators Robert Dole and Phil Gramm, Lamar Alexander, and several others—will need to raise in the neighborhood of ten million dollars before the Iowa caucuses, given the crush of big state events following shortly after the smaller early states.

If money has such a profound impact now, it probably will be even more the case with a national primary event. If nomination politics already has become too heavily driven by sound bite and advertising strategies, it would be even more so with a national primary. Do the improvements in fairness outweigh these detractions?

That is debatable, but the current arrangement should be reformed in such a way as to address its weaknesses and the developments pundits have noted that are making it more and more like a national event, without discarding its good qualities. In particular, efforts should be made to enhance the current arrangement's tendency to encourage some retail politicking, to maintain the possibility of making a candidacy viable without having to raise exorbitant sums of money, and to enable candidates to learn about voters and voters to learn about candidates.

Fixing the Dead Spots

In looking at these reform proposals, the only reasonable conclusion is that the three alternatives either should not or can not be adopted. This conclusion, however, should not be viewed as an endorsement of the current process. The current arrangements are beset with some devastating flaws.

Essentially, none of the comprehensive reform alternatives merits adoption for two reasons. First, the options have enough shortcomings (in the case of regional primaries, a preponderance of them) to make one pause before endorsing such a comprehensive change. The regional primaries reform and the national primary would have the effect of exacerbating some of the weaknesses of the current process, particularly the emphasis on money and mass media sound bite politics. The convention/national primary reform would limit choice in a way that likely would be viewed by many as unacceptable, and, in spite of its many advantages, is a reform that is so against the grain of the evolving structure of the parties as to be entirely unrealistic. Second, the weaknesses of the current arrangements can be addressed with imaginative reforms that would not destroy, and in some cases would enhance, the notable strengths the current process has.

The current arrangement has several qualities worth preserving or reviving. One of these is the accessibility of the process to candidates without vast sums of money. While money matters (something that regrettably seems increasingly to be the case), and the candidate with the most has a decided advantage, candidates with modest bankrolls can get noticed and become contenders based on showings in small states that are not prohibitively expensive to campaign in. Also, this small state campaigning brings to the process the opportunity for retail, grass-roots campaigning to an extent not possible in a national primary or even in regional primaries. Most important, a process of discrete, serialized elections uniquely gives voters an opportunity to learn about the candidates for president as the campaign progresses. Voters have been shown to develop fairly sophisticated understandings of the candidates' ideological stances and career accomplishments, and they have the opportunity to make judgments about character, given a sufficient amount of time to digest information.

Having said that, it is no secret that there are several profound problems with the current process, some of which threaten the very advantages described in the previous paragraph. Three of the most serious difficulties are the following:

1. The failure of the process to satisfy the neutrality criterion, effectively producing an electoral process with a regular and repeated bias in favor of certain types of candidates.
2. The considerable potential for violations of the Condorcet criterion (especially in early states), resulting in the potential for momentum to be generated for candidates who are undeserving.
3. The continuing process of the front-loading of primaries, which results in the exacerbation of the Condorcet criterion violation and constitutes a threat to the strengths (accessibility to candidates without huge bankrolls, the opportunity for voters to get a feel for and assess candidates, and the opportunity for voters to reassess the viable candidates in later states) of a serialized nomination process.

This section proposes a set of reforms of the current process that would address these three shortcomings. These reforms are further designed to preserve or strengthen the positive aspects of the process.

The Geographical Balance Plan

The aim of the Geographical Balance Plan is to reduce the emphasis on and impact of Iowa and New Hampshire, while maintaining the advantages that come with small or medium-sized states starting the delegate selection process. In other words, the potential advantage of this plan is that it makes the early tests more neutral, without resorting to some event so large as to preclude retail campaigning and to be beyond the budgets of most candidates.

The main objectives of this reform are: (1) There should be a neutral battleground to test the candidates, (2) the battleground state or states should not be so large as to preclude retail politics, and (3) the battleground state or states should not be so large such that a sweep by any one candidate would make inevitable the nomination of the winner without the proper and reasonable opportunity for voters in later states to reconsider the judgments on the candidates of voters in early states based on new information and more careful processing of existing information.

The most difficult of these objectives to accomplish is the first one. Neutrality technically will be violated with any state or set of states (short of a national event) coming first. The Geographical Balance Plan aims for less skew or more neutrality. The key is not to have the same states with the same idiosyncrasies starting the process and serving as the first test. It would provide for a more neutral arrangement if it were possible to shift the first big test to different states *depending on the field of candidates*, so that no particular candidate has an advantage over the other candidates. The Geographical Balance Plan offers this sort of flexibility.

The basic idea is to have five small to medium-sized states all hold their primaries on the first day of the delegate selection process. The five states would be in different regions of the country. The specific five states that start the process could vary from year to year. To illustrate how the plan would work to improve the neutrality of the first event in the delegate selection process, consider the following imaginary scenario using the candidates from the 1988 Democratic presidential nomination campaign.

For the sake of argument, imagine that Iowa, New Hampshire, North Carolina, Oregon, and Arizona all hold primaries on the first day of the campaign in 1988. The candidates in the Democratic race are Governor Michael Dukakis of Massachusetts, Senator Albert Gore of Tennessee, Reverend Jesse Jackson, former Arizona Governor Bruce Babbitt, the junior Illinois Senator Paul Simon, Representative Richard Gephardt of Missouri, and former Colorado Senator Gary Hart.

The news media, given the choice and opportunity, would not publicize to a great extent an expected victory—for example, an early win in a candidate's home state. The media seems to have gotten more discriminating in this regard in recent years. For example, in 1992 Senator Harkin's victory in Iowa was given almost no attention. Even victories in states that are contiguous to a candidate's home state can be considered "expected" by the media. Such wins get relatively little attention if there are several events in the same week competing for attention, especially if the events are in different regions of the country. For example, consider that Nebraska Senator Bob Kerrey's victory in South Dakota in 1992 was given relatively little attention given the existence that week of several other contests.

When there is only one major test, however, as is the case now with Iowa in the first event and New Hampshire alone shortly thereafter, regional candidates who win seem to receive a considerable amount of attention since that event is the only game in town. Dukakis's 1988 victory in New Hampshire might well have been ignored by the media had more neutral tests been available for coverage that week. The same might be true of Senator Dole's 1988 win in Iowa or of Paul Tsongas's New Hampshire victory in 1992. The media might wisely have given these contests short shrift had there been races in other states in which no candidate had a natural edge.

Based on this sort of thinking, in the imaginary scenario New Hampshire in 1988 would be left to Dukakis, Iowa to Simon and Gephardt, North Carolina to Gore, and Arizona to Babbitt. Iowa would be a crucial test for the two candidates coming from that region of the country, but the state that would receive the most attention because of its regional neutrality would be Oregon. Naturally Oregon has its own biases; Robert Kennedy complained twenty-five years ago that the state had few racial minorities and blue-collar workers, groups that came out to vote for him in large numbers. But the important point is that none of the existing candidates would have a natural regional advantage there. Oregon would not be perfectly neutral, but it would be far more so than Iowa or New Hampshire given the field of contenders.

It is important to note that, *in the view of the media* the state would be the key early test for the Democrats. As a result, the attentive political community, including candidates, consultants, other elites, and members of the public would focus on the results from that relatively *neutral* state. Candidates probably would be stigmatized and maybe eliminated from the race for the nomination because of a loss there, but no candidate would be eliminated by a loss in a state that had a regionally advantaged candidate.

If the scenario is altered to imagine that Dukakis had chosen not to run in 1988, then New Hampshire and Oregon would have been the key early tests. Remember that each of these states was chosen because of its accessibility in terms of population and cost. North Carolina would have emerged as a testing ground had Gore not run, and so on. Candidates would then, on the first day of delegate selection, be tested for their vote-getting skills in a part of the country that is less familiar to them. It would be valuable information for the elites and the public to know which candidates have appeal outside of their home regions.

The following are possible regional categories from which to choose the five states that would start the nomination campaign. One state could be chosen from each region, on a revolving basis from election year to election year. Some states should be exempted from consideration because of the size of the population and the high cost of their media markets. These qualities make the states inaccessible to candidates and render retail politicking difficult or impossible. Certainly the three largest states, California, Texas, and New York, would be ruled out; also the five next largest states, Michigan, Ohio, Pennsylvania, Illinois, and Florida, should be removed from consideration as early testing grounds. Hawaii and Alaska should be removed from consideration because of their remote locations. The result is five regions of eight states each from which to choose the early tests. For the most part the groupings retain regional integrity, although both Tennessee and Arkansas have ended up outside what might be considered their natural regional category.

Northeast: Rhode Island, Delaware, New Jersey, Maine, Vermont, New Hampshire, Massachusetts, Connecticut

South/Atlantic: Mississippi, Alabama, Maryland, Georgia, South Carolina, North Carolina, Virginia, Louisiana

Industrial and Midwest: Tennessee, Missouri, Kentucky, West Virginia, Indiana, Wisconsin, Iowa, Minnesota

Plains and Southwest: Nebraska, Kansas, Oklahoma, North Dakota, South Dakota, Arizona, New Mexico, Arkansas

West: Oregon, Washington, Colorado, Montana, Wyoming, Utah, Nevada, Idaho

This reform, while not eliminating, does significantly lessen the violation of neutrality that exists now, while maintaining the advantages of starting the campaign in affordable states that are not too heavily populated. Also, the number of delegates at stake on the first day would not be so great that any one candidate could effectively clinch the nomination with five victories without giving voters in later states the opportunity to reconsider the judgments of the "first day" electorate. The geographical balance reform would make the process much fairer than it is, without taking away the advantages of the current system.

Of course, the Geographical Balance Plan is not the first attempt to rectify the overemphasis on Iowa and New Hampshire in presidential nomination politics. In fact, one of the main objectives of the popular reform alternatives considered in depth in this book, the national primary, convention/national primary, and regional primaries, is to reduce the emphasis on these two states.

The Geographical Balance Plan is preferable to these options for many reasons. There are advantages inherent in having an accessibly sized early test. Essentially, the retail politicking gives voters a chance to consider the candidates more carefully. Voters have been shown to learn about previously little-known candidates over the course of a nomination campaign—this would be impossible in a one-day event such as a national primary, and starting with a large venue (like a ten-state regional event with large and small states) would make it impossible for many candidates to get a fair hearing. This opportunity for candidates to get a fairer hearing is a good thing for its own sake, but also it is important to note that the parties have a stake in permitting their various factions to have a fair chance to be heard in the public forum of primaries and precinct caucuses to minimize the potential for serious disruptions at their conventions.

An advantage of the Geographical Balance Plan is that the first day's events, while important, would not be determinative of the party's nomination. Having a large early test, such as a regional primary, would have the undesirable effect of providing potentially conclusive results with a very large field of contenders. As has been shown, in large fields of candidates electoral results are particularly unreliable. It is better to have small early states gradually weed out candidates so that later larger contests with hundreds of delegates at stake (either big states or multistate primary days) are not contested by too many candidates. The simple point is that electoral results are not technically reliable with large fields of candidates, particularly fields greater than three. In presidential primaries, the early states frequently have more than three candidates.

Thus, small early tests are useful for the voters in narrowing down the field of candidates to a manageable number, and they are useful to the parties in identifying the stronger candidates. But it is very unwise to structure a nomination process to provide conclusive results (either in a regional event or a national primary) when the number of candidates is large.

The nomination process should maintain the concept of small states leading the process, so that some voters have the opportunity to see and evaluate candidates up close and other voters have the opportunity to reevaluate the decisions of the voters in the first big test. But it is clearly preferable to have the first big test on a neutral battleground. The Geographical Balance plan achieves that.

One advantage of this reform is that it need not be comprehensive. In fact, all of the states do not have to participate in the way suggested earlier. The only requirement is that there be diversity on the opening primary day—it even could be stipulated that Iowa and New Hampshire retain opening day privileges, but these privileges would have to be shared with three other small or medium-sized states. It is a geographically balanced and accessible way to start out the nomination process. The parties should see virtue in it because it provides a neutral early site in which to evaluate the contenders. Political muscle and media hype then could be thrown around based on a result more meaningful than that which comes out of the states that have copped the pole position in recent years and decades. The reform is far superior to the regional primary and the national primary.

Attacking the Other Problems

There are two serious problems still unaddressed by the Geographical Balance Plan. The result from Oregon (the imaginary neutral test in the 1988 Democratic race) still would be tainted with the Condorcet violation in such a large field of candidates. Also, if front-loading continues apace, many of the large states would have moved up to the weeks immediately following the five state kick-off day, and candidates might not have the time to raise money to compete in them after doing well in the first event. This would leave the field of serious contenders to those who could amass a huge bankroll ahead of the primary season.

The following two reforms are designed to address those two problems.

Approval Voting

Perhaps the greatest failing of the current nomination process as a democratic means to select presidential candidates is the great potential for a Condorcet criterion violation. The single-vote method of voting, particularly when the field of candidates exceeds three, has a distressingly low Condorcet efficiency.

The field of candidates is usually greater than three only in the early states. Noncompetitive candidates are quickly weeded out or marginalized after just a few primaries. But the tremendous impact of these early states, in spite of the limited number of delegates at stake, makes the outcomes there matters of considerable normative concern for social choice theorists.

Essentially, candidates are made viable based on early wins in these states, and losing candidates who do not have many resources are relegated to the sidelines in the race for the nomination on the basis of these outcomes. The important point is that the outcome of races for presidential nominations may hinge on a highly problematical method of aggregating voters' preferences.

The Condorcet problem ceases to be an issue after the first few events, since the field of candidates typically becomes so small and single-vote has a high Condorcet efficiency with three voters and 100 percent efficiency with two. But those candidates may have survived *because* of the faulty method of aggregating preferences. The momentum generated for winners in the early states may lead to successes that are wholly undeserved.

A minor and simple reform would lead to a great improvement in the nomination process as a method of public choice. Approval voting in the initial five-state primaries (or in New Hampshire in the current arrangements) would greatly increase the chance that deserving candidates would enjoy the fruits of early success and that undeserving candidates would not. Giving the voters the opportunity to express a preference for any candidate of whom they approve in these early states that commonly have large multicandidate fields would greatly enhance democracy. The dynamics of momentum inexorably work their magic at that point. There would be no need for later states to use approval when only two or three alternatives are given voters.

Ending Front-loading

The process of front-loading is the most imminent worsening problem confronting today's presidential nomination process as a worthwhile institution of public choice. In a nutshell, everything good about the current arrangement is jeopardized by the once gradual, and now quickening, movement of primaries to the front of the window.

To start with, front-loading has put so many primaries early in the year that candidates who do well in early states have no opportunity to capitalize on these successes by raising more money before the next wave of primaries occurs. In effect, the advantage held by well-heeled candidates is increased with front-loading. Candidates who can raise ten or more million dollars are the only ones who can be competitive when so many prohibitively expensive primaries are scheduled in the early part of the campaign.

Perhaps even more important, more than a thousand delegates will be selected within just a few weeks as the 1996 process seems to be shaping up. This means that voters in many states, many of them quite large, will have gotten no opportunity to learn about the candidates before their states' primaries. Bartels convincingly shows that voters do learn important things about candidates' issue positions and character—but they must be given several weeks to digest information to make this a realistic opportunity.

The most important ramification of this is that the dynamics of the front-loaded campaign likely will make the nomination a fait accompli very early, perhaps even in March. By the time voters have learned about the candidates, most candidates no longer will be viable. As was mentioned in chapter 1, a hastily made choice from a field of candidates that in some years is made up largely of unknown political figures is no way to select a commander in chief. Only in the United States is there institutionalized a method of executive selection that offers the distinct possibility that a person known only to a small fraction of the public and not endorsed by the regular party can win a party's nomination.

The greatest advantage of serialized primaries (sufficiently spread out across the calendar) is that voters in later states have the opportunity to reconsider the choices made by the early state voters. This can occur after voters have become relatively sophisticated about the candidates. New information invariably comes out, and later state voters can make a more sober choice from among the remaining alternatives.

The way the process is becoming, no such opportunity will exist. In effect, the nominees of the major parties to be the next leader of the free world might be decided in a brief period in late February and March, without any reasonable chance to reconsider by voters. It all happens very quickly, and as recent history has shown, a person who was all but unknown up until February of the election year can vault himself into a major party nomination on the basis of victories in a whirlwind of primaries in the late winter.

Oddly enough, front-loading is not a difficult problem to fix. The national parties do have the power to make the following simple change. They should limit the number of primaries that may be scheduled in any week for the six week period following the New Hampshire primary. No more than five primaries and precinct-level caucuses should be permitted during any one week. (The parties could resolve conflicts by lottery or by rotating places on the calendar among the states from election year to election year.) This would end front-loading and all the dangers inherent in it and would permit voters the opportunity to survey the field of candidates before huge numbers of delegates were chosen.

What Does the Future Hold?

For better or worse the major U.S. political parties are committed to intraparty democracy in the selection of their presidential candidates. The institution of public choice in presidential nomination politics must afford the public the opportunity to make a wise choice in selecting the major candidates to be the next chief executive.

The three reforms outlined here address the major shortcomings of the existing presidential nomination process. The Geographical Balance Plan would level the playing field—in social choice terminology, it mitigates the neutrality violation inherent in serialized elections. Approval voting improves the Condorcet efficiency of primaries that are likely to have more than three contenders. Limiting the number of primaries that can be held in any one week allows for a superior quality of decision making by the public during the delegate selection phase of the campaign. Any one of these reforms improves the current arrangements; taken together they would constitute a significant advance.

It is important to take a step back to look at what is taking place in presidential nomination politics in the mid-1990s. The importance of these events cannot be overstated. In presidential primaries, the American people are participating directly in the selection of the two likely alternatives to be the next president of the United States. And it is the case that one of these nominees, in becoming the next president, will have control over the greatest military and nuclear arsenal in the world. Needless to say, this is a process that must be taken seriously.

It is a process that can, and has, made someone a major party nominee and subsequently president who was all but unknown less than a year before he was to become president. Common sense dictates that the public be wary of making the commander-in-chief a person about whom nothing was known such a short time before. No other country selects its major party nominees for chief executive positions in any way even vaguely resembling the U.S. process, at least in part because of a desire to select a well-known person who has served the country with distinction over the course of years or decades.

The U.S. process, on the other hand, is very open, and it is likely to be retained rather than reinstituting peer review in a closed party-dominated framework. How this peculiar electoral procedure is arranged has profound consequences. As a result, how this process of direct democracy is set up should be considered very carefully. This book is predicated on the notion that the parties have made an all but irrevocable commitment to direct forms of democracy at all levels of politics. The aim is to provide the tools to understand the evolution and development of this commitment in recent years, as well as some tools to analyze better the quality of the presidential nomination process, and to provide alternatives to correct its worst excesses.

As long as the Democratic and Republican parties continue to dominate U.S. politics, at the presidential level and all other levels, to the exclusion of any new parties or independent candidacies, it is a sure bet that they will not institute any changes to their commitment to direct democracy in nomination politics. It would take a momentous shake-up of the party system to alter what has evolved in the course of this century in the internal politics of the two parties.

Having said that, momentous shake-ups in the party system *have* happened in the past. Scholars call these shake-ups *realignments.* In the 1820s, in the 1860s, in the 1890s, in the 1930s, and in the 1960s the U.S. party system underwent significant upheavals. At roughly regular intervals the two parties have become unsatisfactory to large numbers of voters. Usually as the result of some developing tension in the polity—an economic crisis or a cultural crisis—that is not being addressed satisfactorily by the parties as they are currently configured, there is a realignment of the party system.

For example, in the 1930s during the Great Depression, the Democratic party benefited from the charisma and foresight of Franklin Roosevelt to convert millions of new and old voters to the Democratic fold, effectively cobbling together a national majority in favor of activist government. Also, in the 1960s and 1970s, Richard Nixon succeeded in redefining the Republicans as the party of cultural conservatism in response to the social tumult of the 1960s and the leftward cultural drift of the Democratic party. This gave the GOP an advantage in presidential politics that lasted for a quarter century.

In the 1990s the discontent with the ways that the two major parties are addressing the cultural and economic issues of the day is palpable. For many Americans the parties have become irrelevant. Small percentages of voters participate in nomination politics, and increasing percentages do not have firm allegiances to either party, and many support the concept of a third party when prompted by pollsters. The independent candidacy of Ross Perot surged ahead of the presumptive Democratic and Republican nominees for president in polls in June of 1992. Even after he demonstrated a tendency toward erratic behavior by dropping in and out of the race, and could not attract any major national figure to be his running mate, he still received almost 20 percent of the vote on election day.

The upshot is that the Democratic and Republican parties run the risk of becoming irrelevant to the political process if they do not address the concerns of the American people in a way that is satisfactory to them. If an independent or third-party candidate were elected or forced an election into the House of Representatives, the existing parties would be forced to rethink their raison d'etre. This rethinking would include, perhaps first and foremost, a restructuring of their method of nominating candidates for president, perhaps including a rethinking of the commitment to plebiscitary legitimation.

This apocalyptic scenario for the parties may or may not happen—surely it still seems like a longshot that anyone other than a Democrat or a Republican could be elected president. These two parties have proven flexible and adaptable time and again in the last 135 years of U.S. political history since the Republican party elected its first president. So barring the eventuality of a successful third-party movement, scholars, journalists, and interested citizens are likely to be arguing the merits and debating potential reforms of the participatory presidential nomination process for some time to come.

Bibliography

Abramson, Paul R., John H. Aldrich, Phil Paolino, and David Rohde (1992) "'Sophisticated' Voting in the 1988 Presidential Primaries," *American Political Science Review* 86: 55–69.

Aldrich, John H. (1980) *Before the Convention.* Chicago: University of Chicago Press.

——— (1980) "A Dynamic Model of Presidential Nomination Campaigns," *American Political Science Review* 74: 651–69.

Arrow, Kenneth (1963) *Social Choice and Individual Values.* 2d ed. New Haven, CT: Yale University Press.

Atkeson, Lonna Rae (1993) "Moving Toward Unity: Attitudes in the Nomination and General Election Stages of a Presidential Campaign." *American Politics Quarterly* 21: 272–89.

Barry, Brian and Russell Hardin, eds. (1982) *Rational Man and Irrational Society?: An Introduction and Sourcebook.* Beverly Hills: Sage Publications.

Bartels, Larry M. (1985) "Expectations and Preferences in Presidential Nomination Campaigns." *American Political Science Review* 79: 804–15.

——— (1988) *Presidential Primaries and the Dynamics of Public Choice.* Princeton: Princeton University Press.

——— (1987) "Candidate Choice and the Dynamics of the Presidential Nomination Process." *American Journal of Political Science* 31: 1–32.

——— (1985) "Resource Allocation in a Presidential Campaign." *Journal of Politics* 47: 928–36.

Beniger, J.R. (1976) "Winning the Presidential Nomination: National Polls and State Primary Elections, 1937–1972." *Public Opinion Quarterly* 40: 22–38.

Blumenthal, Sidney (1982) *The Permanent Campaign*, New York, NY: Simon and Shuster.

Brady, Henry E., and Stephen Ansolabeherre (1989) "The Nature of Utility Functions in Mass Publics." *American Political Science Review* 83: 143–64.

Brady, Henry E., and Richard Johnston (1987) "What's the Primary Message: HorseRace or Issue Journalism?" *Media and Momentum.* In Gary R. Orren and Nelson W. Polsby. Chatham, N.J.: Chatham House Publishers, 127–86.

Brams, Steven J. and Peter C. Fishburn (1983) *Approval Voting*, Boston: Birkhauser.

——— (1982) "Polls and the Problem of Strategic Information and Voting Behavior." *Society* 19: 4–11.

——— (1978) *The Presidential Election Game*, New Haven: Yale University Press.

Buell, Emmett H., Jr. (1986) "Divisive Primaries and Participation in Fall Presidential Campaigns: A Study of 1984 New Hampshire Primary Activists." *American Politics Quarterly* 14: 376–90.

Burnham, Walter D. (1970) *Critical Elections and the Mainsprings of American Politics*, New York: Norton.

Cavala, William (1974) "Changing the Rules Changes the Game: Party Reform and the 1972 California Delegation to the Democratic National Convention." *American Political Science Review* 68: 27–42.

Ceaser, James W. (1979) *Presidential Selection*, Princeton: Princeton University Press.

——— (1982) *Reforming the Reforms*, Cambridge, Mass.: Ballinger Publishing Company.

Collat, Donald S., Stanley Kelley, Jr., and Ronald Rogowski (1981) "The End Game in Presidential Nominations." *American Political Science Review* 75: 426–35.

Congressional Quarterly Weekly Report, 32 (1974); 36 (1978); 40 (1982).

Crotty, William J. and John S. Jackson (1985) *Presidential Primaries and Nominations*, Washington, D.C.: Congressional Quarterly Press.

Doron, Gideon and Richard Kronick (1977) "Single Transferable Vote: An Example of a Perverse Social Choice Function." *American Journal of Political Science* 21: 303–11.

Downs, Anthony (1957) *An Economic Theory of Democracy*, New York: Harper and Row.

Edsall, Thomas B. (1984) *The New Politics of Inequality*, New York: W. W. Norton.

Ehrenhalt, Alan (1991) *The United States of Ambition: Politicians, Power, and the Pursuit of Office.* 1st ed., New York: Times Books.

Epstein, Leon (1978) "Political Science and Presidential Nominations." *Political Science Quarterly* 93: 177–89.

Fishburn, Peter C., and Steven J. Brams (1981) "Approval Voting, Condorcet's Principle, and Runoff Elections." *Public Choice* 36: 89–114.

Geer, John G. (1989) *Nominating Presidents*, New York: Greenwood Press.

——— (1988) "Assessing the Representativeness of Electorates in Presidential Primaries." *American Journal of Political Science* 32: 929–45.

Gopoian, J. David (1982) "Issue Preferences and Candidate Choice in Presidential Primaries." *American Journal of Political Science* 26: 523–46.

Greenfield, Jeff (1982) *The Real Campaign*, New York: Summitt Books.

Gurian, Paul—Henri (1986) "Resource Allocation Strategies in Presidential Nomination Campaigns." *American Journal of Political Science* 30: 802–21.

Hadley, Arthur T. (1976) *The Invisible Primary*, Englewood Cliffs, N.J.: Prentice—Hall.

Haskell, John (1992) "The Paradox of Plebiscitary Democracy in Presidential Nomination Campaigns." *Western Political Quarterly* 45: 1001–19.

Hess, Stephen (1978) *The Presidential Campaign*. Washington, D.C.: The Brookings Institution.

Keech, William and Donald Matthews (1976) *The Party's Choice*. Washington, D.C.: The Brookings Institution.

Keeter, Scott and Cliff Zukin (1983) *Uninformed Consent*. New York: Praeger.

Kenney, Patrick J. and Tom Rice (1987) "The Relationship Between Divisive Primaries and General Election Outcomes." *American Journal of Political Science* 31: 31–44.

——— (1994) "The Psychology of Political Momentum." *Political Research Quarterly* 47: 923–38.

Kessell, John H. (1984) *Presidential Campaign Politics*, Homewood, Ill.: Dorsey Press.

Kirkpatrick, Jeane (1975) "Representation in the American National Convention." *British Journal of Political Science* 5: 265–322.

Lengle, James I. (1980) "Divisive Presidential Primaries and Party Electoral Prospects, 1932–1976." *American Politics Quarterly* 8: 261–77.

——— (1981) *Representation and Presidential Primaries: the Democratic Party in the Post Reform Era*. WestportConn.: Greenwood Press.

Lengle, James I., and Byron E. Shafer (1976) "Primary Rules, Political Power, and Social Change." *American Political Science Review* 70: 25–40.

Lengle, James I., Diana Owen, and Molly W. Sonner (1995) "Divisive Nominating Mechanisms and Democratic Party Electoral Prospects." *Journal of Politics* 57: 370–83.

Lowi, Theodore J. (1985) *The Personal President*. Ithaca, N.Y.: Cornell University Press.

Lucy, William (1973) "Polls, Primaries, and Presidential Nominations." *Journal of Politics* 35: 830–48.

Mandate for Reform (1970) Washington, D.C.: Democratic National Committee.

Marshall, Thomas R. (1981) *Presidential Nominations in a Reform Age.* New York: Praeger.

Mayhew, David R. (1986) *Placing Parties in American Politics.* Princeton: Princeton University Press.

Merrill, Samuel III (1988) *Making Multicandidate Elections More Democratic.* Princeton: Princeton University Press.

Milkis, Sidney M. and Michael Nelson (1990) *The American Presidency: Origins and Development, 1776–1990.* Washington, D.C.: CQ Press.

Nelson, Michael, ed (1989). *Congressional Quarterly's Guide to the Presidency.* Congressional Quarterly Inc.; Washington D.C.

Niemi, Richard G. (1984) "The Problem of Strategic Behavior Under Approval Voting." *American Political Science Review* 78: 952–58.

Niemi, Richard G., and Larry M. Bartels (1984) "The Responsiveness of Approval Voting to Political Circumstances." *PS* 17: 571–77.

Norrander, Barbara, and Gregg Smith (1985) "Type of Contest, Candidate Strategy, and Turnout in Presidential Primaries." *American Politics Quarterly* 13: 28–50.

———— (1989) "Ideological Representativeness of Presidential Primary Voters." *American Journal of Political Science* 33: 570—87.

———— (1991) "Patterns of Voting in the Super Tuesday Primaries: Momentum and Ideology." Presented at the annual meeting of the Western Political Science Association, Seattle.

———— (1992) *Super Tuesday: Regional Politics and Presidential Primaries.* Lexington, Ky.: University of Kentucky Press.

———— (1993) "Nomination Choices: Caucus and Primary Outcomes, 1976–1988." *American Journal of Political Science* 37: 343–64.

Orren, Gary R., and Nelson W. Polsby (1987) *Media and Momentum*, Chatham, N.J.: Chatham House Publishers.

Parent, T. Wayne, Calvin C. Jillson, and Ronald E. Weber (1987) "Voting Outcomes in the 1984 Democratic Party Primaries and Caucuses." *American Political Science Review* 81: 67–84.

Patterson, Thomas E. (1980) *The Mass Media Election*. New York: Praeger.

Polsby, Nelson W. (1983) *Consequences of Party Reform*. New York: Oxford University Press.

Price, David E. (1984) *Bringing Back the Parties*. Washington, D.C.: Congressional Quarterly Press.

Ranney, Austin (1972) "Turnout and Representation in Presidential Primary Elections." *American Political Science Review* 66: 21–42.

———— (1975) *Curing the Mischiefs of Faction: Party Reform in America*, Berkeley: University of California Press.

———— (1978) *The Federalization of Presidential Primaries*. Washington, D.C.: American Institute for Public Policy Research.

Reiter, Howard L. (1985) *Selecting the President*. Philadelphia: University of Pennsylvania Press.

"Report of the Commission on the Democratic Selection of Presidential Nominees." *Congressional Record* . 90th Cong., 2d session, 1968. Vol. 114, pt. 24.

Riker, William H. (1980) "Implications from the Disequilibrium of Majority Rule for the Study of Institutions." *American Political Science Review* 74: 432–46.

———— (1982) *Liberalism Against Populism*. San Francisco: W.H. Freeman.

Sabato, Larry J. (1988) *The Party's Just Begun*. Boston: Scott Foresman.

———— (1981) *The Rise of Political Consultants*. New York: Basic Books.

Sanford, Terry (1981) *A Danger of Democracy*. Boulder, Colo.: Westview

Press.

Schattschneider, E. E. (1960) *The Semisovereign People: A Realist's View of Democracy in America.* New York: Holt, Rinehart, and Winston.

Schlesinger, Joseph A. (1975) "The Primary Goals of Political Parties." *American Political Science Review* 69: 840—49.

——— (1984) "On the Theory of Party Organization." *Journal of Politics* 46: 840—49.

——— (1985) "The New American Political Party." *American Political Science Review* 79: 1152–69.

Seligman, Lester G., and Cary R. Covington (1989) *The Coalitional Presidency.* Chicago: Dorsey Press.

Shafer, Byron E. (1983) *Quiet Revolution*, New York, NY: Russell Sage Foundation.

——— (1988) *Bifurcated Politics: Evolution and Reform in the National Party Convention.* Cambridge, Mass: Harvard University Press.

Stone, Walter J. (1984) "Prenomination Candidate Choice and General Election Behavior: Iowa Presidential Activists in 1980." *American Journal of Political Science* 28: 361–78.

Stone, Walter J., Ronald B. Rapoport, and Alan I. Abrahamowitz (1992) "Candidate Support in Presidential Nomination Campaigns: The Case of Iowa in 1984." *Journal of Politics* 54: 1074–97.

Stone, Walter J., Lonna Rae Atkeson, and Ronald B. Rapoport (1992) "Turning On or Turning On? Mobilization and Demobilization Effects of Participation in Presidential Nomination Campaigns." *American Journal of Political Science* 36: 665–91.

The Wall Street Journal. December 4, 1987.

Witcover, Jules (1977) *Marathon, the Pursuit of the Presidency, 1972–1976.* New York: Viking Press.

Yu, Peter M. (1987) "By the Numbers: A Statistical Profile of New Hampshire." In Gary R. Orren and Nelson W. Polsby, *Media and Momentum.* Chatham, N.J.: Chatham House Publishers, 187–95.

Index

About the Author

John Haskell is Associate Professor of Political Science at Drake University. His work has appeared in *Western Political Quarterly, Who Runs for Congress?* (Congressional Quarterly), and *Presidential Studies Quarterly* (forthcoming, 1997).